Persons, Mind and Value

Utkal Studies in Philosophy

General Editor

P.K. Mohapatra

Editors

T. Patnaik, S.K. Mohanty
G.P. Das, S.C. Panigrahi

Volume One
Action, Freedom and Responsibility

Volume Two
God, Time and Evil

Volume Three
Studies on the Mysticism

Volume Four
Reality and Mysticism

Volume Five
Social Justice

Volume Six
Facets of Humanism

Volume Seven
Varnadharma, Niskama Karma
and Practical Morality

Volume Eight
Persons, Mind and Value

Utkal Studies in Philosophy - VIII
General Editor: P.K. Mohapatra

Persons, Mind and Value

Editor
S.K. Mohanty

Decent Books, New Delhi
in association with
Department of Special Assistance in Philosophy
Utkal University, Bhubaneswar

Published and Printed by:
Decent Books
D-36/A-1, Mohan Garden
Najafgarh Road
New Delhi - 110 059

Distributed by:
D.K. Printworld (P) Ltd.
Regd. office : '*Sri Kunj*', F-52, Bali Nagar
New Delhi - 110 015
Phones : (011) 545-3975, 546-6019; *Fax* : (011) 546-5926
E-mail: dkprint@4mis.com

ISBN 81-86921-07-9

First Published in India in 1999

From the General Editor

The present volume is the result of a project undertaken by our Special Assistance Programme. As a part of this project, Professor B.H. Boruah of I.I.T., Kanpur worked as a Visiting Fellow in this Department in December 1996 and delivered a series of lectures on the theme "Persons, Mind and Value". His lectures incited considerable interest and it was felt that there is much to think about and debate over the issues raised by Boruah's thought provoking lectures. Subsequently, Professors R.C. Pradhan and Amitabha Das Gupta of the University of Hyderabad, both Visiting Fellows at Utkal at different times, worked on this project and delivered lectures on the theme. Chapters 2 and 3 comprise their contributions. The present volume is thus a useful outcome of this collaborative effort. Chapter 4 is written by Dr. S.K. Mohanty who has painstakingly taken up the task of editing this volume with this very relevant contribution.

The philosophical accounts of personhood have been often used for building normative ethical theories. Many philosophers think that values have their source in persons and the concept of a person is deeply embedded in moral discourse. The contributions to this book have explored the link between persons and value. In so far as persons and value are linked to mentality of the subject, relevant features of mind have been brought into focus.

The concept of a person has received a good deal of recent attention by philosophers, psychologists, neuroscientists and computer scientists. In the past the concept mainly figured in the discussion on the criterion of personal identity and survival after death. It was also debated whether non-physical beings like angels and God can be treated as persons. In recent times the concept has acquired greater philosophical significance due to a variety of reasons. Some of these are as follows. When we think of persons, we have in mind normal adult human beings. Yet the two notions are not synonymous. The concept of a person is basically a psychological concept whereas the concept of human being is a biological one. Even if most human beings satisfy the requirements of personhood, one must admit the possibility of non-human persons as well as human non-persons. Locke's allusion to an 'intelligent parrot' is an important pointer. One source of this recognition comes from the progressing displacement of humanity through the work of Darwin and other biologists who point out that human species differ only in degree and not in kind from higher animals. There is no biologically or psychologically privileged position of the human species as a whole. Concern for human species has been branded as anthropocentric parochialism or human chauvinism. The minimal feature of personhood which are found in human species can be located in other higher animals as well. Another source of challenge to the privileged status of human beings comes from computer generated agents like the chess playing intelligent machine, Deep Blue, and the possibility of artificial persons in the form of robotic creatures, zombies, who can be functionally equivalent to human persons and demand to be treated with dignity and respect. The question naturally arises, are there any features of personhood that cannot be instantiated by higher animals on the one hand and artificial robotic creatures on the other?

The contributions to this volume explore the concept of personhood as a source of value. B.H. Boruah's paper undertakes a philosophical exercise in moral psychology, with the hope that philosophical analysis and elucidation of the psychological structure of moral agency can illuminate issues in moral theory. He shows the intimate link between persons and value by analysing the notion of mental subjectivity, ontology of personhood and the motivational structure of the mental life of a person. Boruah analyses the notion of moral personhood by examining the nature of personal consciousness, person-constitutive attitudes and the dialectical interplay of the motivational and evaluative elements within the psyche of the agent. He argues the moral personhood can be analysed and articulated only from the first-person perspective. He holds that mental subjectivity can be explicated in terms of the phenomenological feature of experience. Highlighting the 'what it is like' to experience, to do and to be something features of the subject, he argues that the subjectivity of the mental cannot be reduced to the objective order of reality. Then he joins issues with physicalism and functionalism — theories which advocate conscious inessentialism.

Boruah further argues that morality is not entirely a matter of pure rationality. In so far as moral agency requires transcendence of ego-centricity, Boruah says, it can be characterised as spiritual. Through self-excellence or self-transcendence the individual realises herself. Freedom, for Boruah, consists in being able to translate our higher-order desires into actual motivations of actions, such that what we *want* is what we *value*. The paper spells out in detail how the notions of spirituality, freedom and rationality are involved in the very concept of moral personhood.

R.C. Pradhan's paper addresses the issues raised in Boruah's paper and further elucidates them. Pradhan emphasises that moral commitment is a necessary feature of moral personhood. He further argues that mere second-order desires are not enough for moral agency. The fact that second-order desires can simply be the mechanical activity of classifying and ordering, an agent may fail to choose the higher order desire if she does not have value commitments. Pradhan insists that the capacity for self-transcendence is the *sine qua non* for moral agents. Pradhan makes the bold assertion that the intrinsic urge for self-transcendence — the urge to seek higher levels of existence, higher levels of consciousness and higher levels of happiness

— leads to the realisation of the cosmic or universal self.

Amitabh Das Gupta points out that traditionally the concept of freedom has been construed in terms of two alternative perspectives — the subjective internal perspective and the objective external perspective. Das Gupta thinks, these perspectives give rise to certain tensions and philosophical perplexities. He questions the internalist perspective of freedom which assumes the fact-value dichotomy. He develops an existential approach to freedom, a freedom as we experience in the world. The freedom as we experience in the world does not recognise the fact-value dichotomy. Das Gupta argues for the thesis of fact-value holism and develops a concept of freedom in existential and situational terms on the basis of fact-value holism.

S.K. Mohanty analyses the concept of a person and draws attention to the fact that there is not one but several conceptions of personhood — at any rate several levels thereof. The minimal sense of personhood relies on the contrast between property and person. Our attitude to persons is different from our attitude to property. Property is something which can be bought or sold, owned or given away. To treat someone as a person is to express our moral concern and recognise him or her intrinsic worth. This concept is often employed to draw the boundary of a moral community whose members are the proper objects of moral concern, beings who make moral claims on us. There is a stronger sense in which the concept of a person has been employed to delineate the class of beings who have special moral claims. Beings who are minimally rational can have morally relevant interests not found in mere sentient beings. There is still a stricter sense when personhood is meant to refer to beings who are rational moral agents, who not only have rights but also have duties and responsibilities. Such beings will be required to have the freedom of choice in a stronger sense. Mohanty argues that the personal stance appropriate to beings who are persons in a stronger sense will not apply to persons understood in a weaker sense. This entails that the nature and content of our moral concern will be different for different levels of personhood.

The editiors wish to thank the authors for their valuable contributions, especially to Professor Boruah to whom belongs the major credit for this volume. The philosophy faculty at Utkal made valuable contributions by their participation and critical observations during the presentations of the lectures; all of them deserve thanks.

We must thank the U.G.C. for their generous grant which made this publication possible. We also thank M/S Decent Books, New Delhi for taking up the publication of this book.

Utkal University **P.K. Mohapatra**
15 October 1998

Contents

1

Person and Value: Sketch for a Theory of Moral Personhood

Bijoy H. Boruah

Introduction

In this paper I attempt to sketch a theory of moral personhood through an analysis of the concept of a human being endowed with the special feature of consciousness. Attention to the features of human consciousness is drawn with respect to two salient aspects of the possibility of attaining moral personality. One aspect is that of consciousness as the source of moral *rationality*, and the qualitative motivational refinement induced by rational consciousness. The other aspect is consciousness as the source of moral *spirituality*, which is the characteristic of the moral person to transcend selfishness or egoism and, thus, to be spiritually motivated to become a 'selfless' self.

As a preliminary step, I take the following three steps for granted:

A. Person is a valuational aspect.
B. Value is an irreducibly normative concept.
C. The reality of value supervenes on the reality of consciousness.

My taking the above steps for granted does not mean that they are unarguably true. However, I shall take up the task of elucidating, rather than proving the truth of, these claims. I shall begin by discussing step C, in which I intend to show that the ontology of values is determined by the ontology of consciousness or mental subjectivity. This discussion will be followed by an account of the nature of persons as self-conscious, rational subjects whose crucial existential status is valuational. This is step A. I shall not take up step B for a separate treatment, but this step will find its elucidation by implication in the overall account.

Elucidation of the idea of mental subjectivity will set the scene for projecting the view that persons are constituted, in essence, by the intersubjective personal stance. This will be discussed in Section 3. Section 4 will analyse the dialectical structure of personhood, that is the process of a personal life which is characterised by the conflict of desires of different order, and regulated by the aim of self-excelling.

The feature of self-excelling encapsulates human freedom as a creative mode of progressive self-regulation.That freedom consists in being able to translate our higher-order desires into actual motivations of actions, such that what we want is what we value, will be the argument of Section 5. This argument directly results in a theory of moral personhood, which is to be articulated in Section 6 in terms of the coordination of a person's system of motivations with a system of evaluation that the person forms in course of self-excelling. Finally, in Section 7, an attempt will be made to establish the claim that, to the extent moral personhood requires transcendence of ego-centricity, or selfishness, moral motivation is ultimately spiritual.

I

Mental Subjectivity

THE LINKED DUALITY

The question of mental subjectivity is about the concept of a mental subject, or the idea of a subject essentially endowed with mental properties. What underlies mentally, and which also sustains the idea of a subject (or subjecthood), is *consciousness*. A conscious being, which is a being characterised by the ability to experience something — pain or pleasure, light or sound, etc. — is, by virtue of this ability (or sentience), a subject. Consciousness underpins subjecthood, and being a subject in this sense means *that there is something which it is like to be* such a being — an organism of some kind at all (Nagel, 1979a).

There is a sense, therefore, in which a mental subject is a conscious organism, of which it is true to say that the organism has a life of awareness *for* itself. The organism, because of its consciousness or awareness, is a being-for-itself rather than a being-in-itself. Subjecthood is the feature of a being whose being is for-itself. The organism is a subject because it is essentially characterised by awareness or consciousness. It would cease to be a subject if its organic constitution did not ensure the possibility of sentience. Conversely, the organism cannot fall to be a subject once its organic constitution is of the kind that generates consciousness, and thereby makes it true that there is something it is like to *be* that organism *for* the organism.

Thus, it seems to be a fundamental truth about any being whatsoever, which has conscious experience of any sort, that having such an experience entails being a subject of that experience. And this must be granted irrespective of views about the *nature* of the subject of experience. It is not a deep truth though, for it is a clear reflection of the simple point that any experience is, necessarily, experience-*for*-someone-or-something. This applies as much to a newborn baby or a spider as it applies to adult humans. Subjecthood therefore is not a prerogative of humans.

What perhaps, *is* a prerogative of humans is the subjecthood that attaches to propositional attitudes, or mental states (both experiential and non-experiential) which have propositional or representational content, such as beliefs, desires, emotions, intentions and so on. Being the subject of a belief or emotion, *for* whom it is the belief or emotion, entails being an organism with a cognitive capacity in virtue of which the subject is able to form a representation of what the belief or emotion is about. Human organisms above the earliest infancy are possessed of this capacity, but it is not clear whether non-human organisms have it as well.

Confining now to the human case, we can safely generalise the above simple but fundamental truth about subjecthood and mental content (both experiential and non-experiential, and with or without representational content) as the following: a subject is one part of the *linked duality* which is the nature of any conscious mental event. This generalisation, in turn, serves as a condensed account of what consciousness consists in. To borrow the words of Ted Honderich, consciousness in general consists in the "interdependent existence of subject and content" where the interdependence is such that "there can be no subject without content, and no contents not in relation to a subject"[1].

Mental content, in the sense explained above, is subjective content. Take the subject away and you also thereby take the mental state inalienably linked to the subject. A pain, for example, is necessarily and inextricably a state of the sufferer, and it has therefore no reality apart from the subjective mode of life of the sufferer. Likewise, a belief or a desire exists only by drawing subjective sustenance from the believing or desiring subject, so to speak. What I truly believe to be a donkey, and which I actually desire to ride on, exists in the objective (hence, extra-subjective) order. But my belief or desire itself exists only in the subjective order of reality. One can rightly characterise this as the *subjectivity feature* of mental phenomena.

The foregoing discussion makes it clear that mental phenomena are subjective in two kinds of way. There is experiential or *phenomenal* subjectivity, that is the subjective

1. T. Honderich, *Mind and Brain*, (Oxford, Clarendon Press, 1988), p. 82.

property states of bodily sensation and perceptual experience. This is the subjectivity of *qualia*. The other is *intentional* subjectivity, that is the non-qualitative subjective property of *representing* in consciousness an actual or putative state of affairs. While phenomenal subjectivity involves the subject's being in a mental state which is intrinsically qualitatively contentful, intentional subjectivity attaches to a mental state of the subject which is intrinsically representationally contentful.

FIRST-PERSON PERSPECTIVE AND PERSPECTIVAL REALISM

The upshot of the preceding discussion is that realism about mental phenomena presupposes the recognition that these phenomena have a subjective mode of being. They are there only as status or events of a conscious subject. It is only from the *point of view* of a subject that they can be given due recognition as real events or states. The *subjective perspective* or the perspective of consciousness, which is what a subject is an embodiment of, makes mental phenomena available as contents of reality. Without that perspective there is no mental reality. Hence mental facts are *perspectival*.

Crucial to the issue of mental subjectivity is the point that the perspective of consciousness is the *first-person* perspective. The perspectival character of mental phenomena therefore implies that mental facts are first-person facts. The first-person factuality of mental facts is as much true of propositional attitudes like belief, desire or intentions as it is true of experiential states like pain or pleasure and perceptual sensations. A pain, for instance, has first-person reality in the sense that it is a pain solely from the experiential point of view of the sufferer. It is not accessible, as an episode of felt experience, from the third-person point of view. Likewise, a belief, for instance, is always a state of a believer's consciousness. It does not float free of that subjective consciousness as a state or event accessible from the third-person point of view. As a state or event, the belief has its reality in the 'subjective field' of an individual consciousness.

What has been argued above is the thesis that realism about mental phenomena is rooted, not in the objectivity of the third-person viewpoint, but in the subjectivity of the first-person perspective. It is the failure to realise this insight that has caught the attention of John Searle, whose emphatic criticism of the objectivist (mis)reading of the nature of the mental drives him to assert that

> much of the bankruptcy of most work in the philosophy of mind and a great deal of sterility of academic psychology . . . have come from a persistent failure to recognise and come to terms with the fact that *the ontology of the mental is an irreducibly first-person ontology*.[2]

Once the idea of first-person ontology is duly connected with the perspective of subjectivity or consciousness, mental reality gets accorded a *sui generis* ontological order, which I have called 'the subjective order' of reality. Mental reality is then clearly not to be mistakenly assessed in terms of criteria of reality appropriate to the objective ontological order.

The objective ontological order carves out the domain of reality containing objects or events which exist mind-independently. The physical universe, for instance, exists independently of anybody's consciousness or thought of it. In this sense of mind-independence we can say that the universe is 'object-ive', meaning thereby that its existence in no way owes to the subjective status of any consciousness. It has object-ive reality. By contrast, mental phenomena, though as real as any objective existent, are real as 'subject-ive' existents. In the senses elucidated here, 'object-ive' and 'subject-ive' are ontological categories to be distinguished from their epistemological counterparts, as when we talk about objective and subjective judgements. The hyphenation above is meant precisely to draw out conspicuously the two senses, ontological and epistemological, and thereby to remove in advance any possible confusion.

---

2. J.R. Searle, *The Rediscovery of the Mind*, Combridge, Massachussetts, Bradford Books/MIT Press, 1992, p. 95 (emphasis added).

The fundamental point that underpins the claim of realism about subjectivity — about subject-ive reality, that is — is that, since reality includes human creatures with the subjectivity feature (of consciousness), there inevitably are phenomena characterised by subject-ive properties as part of the fabric of reality. But, unlike object-ive properties, which are there irrespective of whether reality includes conscious subjects or not, subject-ive properties are conceptually dependent on the existence and continuation of consciousness. The idea of a subject-ive property would be unintelligible without any connection with its correlative idea of a consciousness-endowed, subjective being.

II

Persons in the Subject-ive Order

RATIONAL SELF-CONSCIOUSNESS

The concept of the subject-ive order is not such as to be tied only to conscious humans. In principle, any beings possessed of the ability to experience and to think would, by this very fact, 'generate' phenomena in the subject-ive order. There may therefore be a subject-ive order of reality correlative to non-human conscious beings. In so far as human persons are concerned, however, being one of them means, in the relevant respect of personhood, having subject-ive properties and living a *personal* life in the subject-ive order. Sensations and emotions, thoughts and other intentional attitudes, are all constitutive of personal life, the life of a particular kind of subjectivity (in the adjectival sense of the word, rather than in its nominal-ontological hyphenated sense). It would therefore be appropriate to say that persons are instantiations of a particular mode of being in the subject-ive order.

A necessary consequence of asserting that being a person is instantiating a certain mode of being in the subject-ive order is that there would be no ontological niche for persons in a purely object-ivist account of reality. But the subjectivity of personal life does not consist merely in having subject-ive properties as such. It rather consists in having certain *specific* subject-ive properties, those which lend an intrinsically personal status to a life of subjectivity. In other words, the subject-ive order of personhood, or what may also be rephrased as 'personal subject-ivity', is characterised by a particular range of features of subject-ivity.

While admittedly, it is most difficult to state all the features of subject-ivity which are both necessary and sufficient for personhood, the following are surely necessary features. It surely is necessary that a person be not just conscious but *self-conscious*, and *rational*. This means that the consciousness a person is endowed with has the peculiarity of being reflective and inseparably tied to the exercise of reasoning.

PERSONAL STANCE

Another necessary feature is that personal consciousness contains within itself a *personal stance* which is adopted by one person towards another who, in turn, must be capable of reciprocating in some way. Someone is a person only in so far as the personal stance is adopted towards her or him (or it), and that someone is naturally disposed, in virtue of her or his personal consciousness, to reciprocrate by adopting the same kind of attitude towards whoever happens to treat her or him in this way. Outside the ambit of reciprocal personal stance there is no space for persons. This means that interpersonal attitudinal space is partially constitutive of personhood. This also explains why, metaphysically speaking, there would be no persons at all in a world described in purely object-ive, i.e., *non*-subject-ive, terms. If this is right, then a very important point comes to the fore, which is that there can be no real understanding of the meaning of the concept of person from a standpoint outside the personal stance.

While there is much else to say about the feature of personal stance on the one hand, and the feature of self-conscious rationality on the other, there is still another feature of personhood that can be explained by reference to the combination of the two above-stated features. In virtue of self-conscious rationality someone is a person to the extent that she or he can be (reflexively) conscious of what she or he does through the exercise of reason. And both are persons inasmuch as they figure in the intersubjective attitudinal space created by the mutual adoption of the reciprocal personal stance. When these two features are related to one another, what follows is that personal consciousness is both *inter*-subjective and *intra*-subjective – that is, both a matter of being conscious of others as persons who, in turn, (normally) reciprocate with the same consciousness, and a matter of being conscious of oneself as a conscious creature of a certain kind. We might describe this feature as *transcendental consciousness* in the sense that personal consciousness both transcends individual, ego-centric consciousness, and is transcendentally aware of one's own first-order consciousness.

VALUATIONAL CONSCIOUSNESS

There is yet another feature of personal consciousness which, though it depends on the other three, is not obviously part of them. It is that persons have *valuational* consciousness; that is, they are conscious of the world, other persons and themselves in terms of moral, aesthetic or religious values. Things *mean* to them in certain ways, as having certain significance. Other persons are *respected* or *treated* as significant selves, expecting others also to adopt the same attitude to oneself. And one treats oneself as an embodiment of significance, as a person who *ought* to live in a meaningful way in the midst of other persons and the world.

Because of the valuational feature, the subject-ive order of personal consciousness is never an order of mere description, or descriptively accountable. Normativity is built into the personal subject-ive order, and to this extent person is a normative concept. In this sense it would be no exaggeration to say that being a person is tantamount to fulfilling a norm — the ideal of personhood. The life of a person therefore deserves evaluative assessment.

Taking these four characteristics of personhood, we can now summarise that a person is a transcendentally conscious, value-sensitive rational being that occupies the intersubjective space of reciprocal personal stance. However, it would seem that this summary statement about personhood smacks of circularity in that it contains the phrase 'personal stance'. Surely to try to say what persons are by adding that they are persons in virtue of adopting the *personal* stance towards one another is to beg the question at issue. But I think the statement can be rendered non-question-begging by an unpacking of the meaning of 'personal stance' in terms that constitute the stance or attitude concerned. It is this task that we must take up now.

III

Personal Stance and the Constitution of Personhood

PERSON-CONSTITUTIVE ATTITUDES

A person is a transcendentally conscious (i.e., self-conscious, or conscious of being conscious), value-sensitive, rational being that occupies the inter-subjective space of reciprocal personal stance. Reciprocal personal stance means a stance or attitude which is adopted by any individual personal consciousness towards other individuals, who reciprocate the same attitude towards the individual subject. A conscious individual *becomes* a person only by figuring within the inter-subjective attitudinal space, i.e., a space created by the mutual adoption of a certain set of attitudes between individuals. Outside the ambit of this distinctive, person-constitutive set of attitudes, there is *no* person, although there may be conscious individuals taxonomically subsumable under the species *homo sapiens*. Thus, Deniel Dennett writes that

> it is not the case that once we have established the objective fact

> that something is a person we treat him or her or it a certain way, but that our treating him or her or it in this certain way is somehow and to some extent constitutive of its being a person.[3]

The above account immediately raises a pair of interrelated questions. (*A*) What is the nature of the person-constitutive attitudes, and how are they to be specified? (*B*) How can the idea of a person be elucidated, without begging the question, by reference to the so-called personal stance? These two questions are interlinked in the sense that an answer to (*B*) must draw upon, and is necessarily available in, whatever can be stated in answer to (*A*). In other words, the above way of defining what a person is can be rendered non-question-begging by an unpacking of the meaning of 'personal stance' in terms which to describe and analyse the specific attitudes that are constitutive of personhood.

Indeed, the personal stance or attitude is not adopted towards a being *after* such a being is identified, as a matter of objective fact, as a person. A particular being does not own the status of a person as a natural fact. There is no natural, objective fact of the matter of personhood in the way there is an objective fact of the matter of being a creature of the human species. The concept of a person is not the concept of a natural kind. This is because, amongst other things, personhood is an attitudinally conferred property instantiated by members of the human species in and through their intersubjective relations.

REACTIVE AND OBJECTIVE ATTITUDES

What does the distinctive person-constitutive stance consist in? It consists in a fairly wide range of attitudes of a quite fundamental kind, which have all been subsumed under the rubric 'reactive attitudes' by Strawson, to whom we owe in essence the idea of the personal stance.

---

3. D.C. Dennett, "Conditions of Personhood", in A. Rorty (ed.), *The Identities of Person* (Berkeles, Los Angeles, London University of California Press, 1976), pp. 177-8.

According to Strawson, there is a certain range of attitudes and responses, called 'reactive' or 'participant' attitudes, such as gratitude, resentment, love and hurt feelings, forgiveness, moral indignation and approbation, which grounds the possibility of our being free and responsible human agents who are involved in interpersonal transaction. We would not be the human persons that we are but for our integration into the reciprocal attitudinal framework of human intersubjectivity.

Thus the personal stance is constituted by the reactive attitudes — attitudes in virtue of which we are engaged with one another in a non-detached way. In contrast, there is the objective attitude, to adopt which towards another human being is, according to Strawson,

> to see him, perhaps as an object of social policy; as a subject of what, in a wide range of senses, might be called treatment; as something certainly to be taken account, perhaps precautionary account, of; to be managed, or handled, or cured or trained; perhaps simply to be avoided.

Strawson continues:

> If your attitude towards someone is wholly objective, then though you may fight him, you cannot quarrel with him; and though you may talk to him, even negotiate with him, you cannot reason with him. You can at most pretend to quarrel or reason with him.[4]

A prominent context in which the objective stance is implicit is the theory of determinism. A deference to determinism induces us to look at persons as causal objects amongst others, all equally placed within the objective world of science, and equally subject to causal explanation from the viewpoint of that objective stance. Thus the human person as a free and responsible agent is subjected by Schlick[5] to explanation in terms of the effect on the agent of practices of praising and

---

4. P.F. Strawson, "Freedom and Resentment" in G. Watson (ed.) *Free will* (Oxford, Oxford Univ. Press, 1982), p. 9.

5. See Moritx Schlick, "When is a Man Responsible?" in his *Problems of Ethics* (New York, Prentice Hall, 1939).

blaming her, i.e., practices of reward and punishment. Following this procedure means treating the agent (oneself or another) as an object to be manipulated or prodded, shouted at or soothed, but not reasoned with.

Given the Strawsonian argument, there is something 'depersonalising' about Schlick's account of the agent's freedom and responsibility. For in this account there is no scope for treating the agent as *deserving* praise or blame for what she does. Any kind of causal manipulation of the agent would undermine the fact that the agent, as a human person, can respond appropriately to our reactions, provided we *do* react appropriately to the agent. And our reacting appropriately to the agent means trying to influence her in such a manner that she herself becomes an agent of the change. But to try to *cause* a change in the agent is to bring about a change in her without arousing her own sense of agency. It is this argument that forms the heart of Strawson's critique of Schilick's account as a wrong *kind* of account arising from an impertinent viewpoint.

Granted that the pertinent viewpoint is that of the reactive attitude when it comes to judging persons as persons, it does not imply that it is *always* impertinent to adopt the objective attitude, whatsoever the human circumstances may be. On the contrary, the participant attitudes sometimes rightly tend to give place to non-participant attitudes, especially when the agent is understood to be incapable of participating in ordinary adult human relationships, whether because of being a young child, or because of being much too deranged. Strawson also talks about the pertinence of adopting the objective attitude towards the normal and the mature as a way of taking refuge from, say, the strains of involvement, or simply out of intellectual curiosity.

The case of the neurotic, who becomes virtually unfit for human intercourse with other persons, is particularly relevant to the question of why our withdrawal of the reactive attitude, and the adoption of the objective attitude, towards her is the right stance. Here taking this stance is motivated by our desire to bring about a change in the neurotic patient which will enable her to re-enter the normal life of participation, of full reciprocity of the reactive attitudes. Shifting to the objective attitude on our part with regard to the patient is prompted by our genuine concern that the patient be cured, so that the strategically chosen objective stance can be withdrawn and we return to the reactive stance.

It would follow from the account that the occasional and strategic departure from the reactive attitude to the objective attitude under special circumstances is itself rooted in a second-order reactive attitude, which is that any human agent deflected from the interpersonal attitudinal space ought to be brought back into the sphere of full reciprocity of reactive attitudes. The reactive attitude, which defines the personal stance, therefore *overrides* any switch-over to the objective attitude, such that there is no genuine human possibility of our being entirely overtaken by the objective attitude, without losing our human identity altogether.

FOLK PSYCHOLOGY VERSUS COGNITIVE SCIENCE

One might wonder in a sceptical vein, whether the personal stance, characterised in reactive-attitudinal terms, persists only because we humans are much too sentimentally disinclined to subject the personal attitudes and feelings — all of which together make up what is known as 'folk psychology' — to the justificatory-theoretical test of objective science. If these attitudes and feelings are really examined from the objective stance of science, such as the stance of determinism in particular, then, as the sceptical argument continues, we would be left with no justifying reason for not giving up the personal stance and adopting the objective stance. Are we not blinded by the soporific influence of antiquarian folk psychology to fail to reorientate ourselves in consonance with the 'modern' ideology of what is fashionably known as 'cognitive science', in which there can only be attitudes consistent with the theory of determinism?

A reasonable rejoinder to the sceptical remark would be to voice the words of Strawson:

> A sustained objectivity of interpersonal attitude, and the human isolation which that would entail, does not seem to be something of which human beings would be capable, even if some general truth were a theoretical ground for it.[6]

And this 'incapability' is not contingent, but rooted in a deeper fact, namely that our commitment to ordinary interpersonal attitudes is

> part of the general framework of human life, not something that can come up for review as particular cases can come up for review within this general framework.[7]

The reactive-attitudinal framework, within which we relate to one another as persons, is a condition of our humanity.

The Strawsonian rejoinder to the sceptical adversary may be reinforced by adding that folk psychology, which encapsulates reactive attitudes and therefore the very idea of a person, is not a discredited theory or a degenerate research programme, as Paul Churchland and Stephen Stich[8] think it is; for it is *not* a theory or programme at all that can come up for review and replacement in the light of some new theory. The fact of the matter is that folk psychology is naturally grounded in our human possibility to *be* persons, and to be persons by way of our spontaneous entry into interpersonal relationships. Becoming persons in this way, or engaging oneself in the social practice of dealing with other human beings in terms of reciprocal personal attitudes, does not depend on one's being initiated to

---

6. See Moritx Schlick, "When is a Man Responsible?" in his *Problems of Ethics*, p. 68.

7. *Ibid.*, p.70.

8. See Churchland, "Eliminative Materialism and the Propositional Attitudes", *Journal of Philosophy*, 78, pp. 67-90 and Stich, *From Folk Psychology to Cognitive Science*: *The Ease Against Belief*, (Cambridge, MA, Bradford Books/MIT Press, 1983).

a theory. Hence the adoption of the personal stance, defined in terms of the reactive-attitudinal framework, is no more a contingent choice on our part, facing the likelihood of abandonment in the light of some theory, than choosing to eat while we are hungry is a contingent desire we have.

Cognitive science, either as a new theory about ourselves or as a research programme, is thus no rival of folk psychology. Nor can it provide justificatory criteria for the reasonableness or otherwise of involvement in reciprocal personal attitudes, because these attitudes are not open for justification in terms of any external criteria.

IV

The Dialectical Structure of Personhood

SELF-ALIENATION

In a very fundamental and yet deep sense, a person is always likely to be questionable to herself. As a person, she is not, as a matter of fact, just a certain kind of being, with certain given desires. Rather, it is non-contingently true about a person that it is somehow up to her what kind of being she is going to **be**. It is a celebrated notion of Heideggar's that human persons are such that their being is in question in their being. Beyond the *de facto* characterisation of the human subject by her goals, desires, and purposes, the subject as a person puts to hereself the *de jure* question:

> Is this the kind of person I ought to be, or really want to be?

Persons are, in the above-described sense, self-reflective evaluators, who are capable of taking seriously the Delphic maxim 'know thyself'. Being a person is a normative, valuational project one engages in by living a life of ceaseless self-appraisal leading to self-transformation. It involves having to *alienate* something of one's own nature — some "person-contingent features of the form of embodiment without which it can have no life"[9]. These 'person-contingent' features are various specific needs and desires, ways of perceiving things, moods and manners and many other dispositions, all of which make up the ground-floor resources of ordinary life.

When self-alienation is experienced, it is experienced mainly as a conflict of ground-floor desires and other pro-attitudes. The conflict arises due to reflective self-evaluation, in which some target-desire appears evaluatively undesirable to the person concerned. That desire or pro-attitude, howsoever compelling it may be, is considered to be alien to oneself inasmuch as one prefers, on normative grounds, to indentify oneself with a character or personality from which that desire or pro-attitude must be absent. Alienation of the first-order character, i.e., the character that is naturally formed by ground-floor desires and pro-attitudes, is thus a paradigm enterprise of persons engaged in the pursuit of being what they really want to be.

SECOND-ORDER VOLITION

The first-order desires that a human person has are, to a large extent, part of her human nature. These are what Nerlich describes as *person-contingent* desires. It is a persisting pattern of first-order desires that constitutes the *basic* nature of a person, i.e., the character of a person. However, humans would not be *persons* were they to have only a basic nature or character, the contents of which are, mostly, first-order desires. For persons are distinguished by the criterion that they have what Harry Frankfurt has called 'second-order desires' — more particularly, second-order *volitions*. The ability to form second-order desires is the ability to adopt higher-order attitudes towards one's first-order desires from a value-centric viewpoint. Second-order desires signify the distinctive character of persons as reflective self-evaluators, and it is in the ability to be evaluatively self-reflective that persons manifest their freedom. Frankfurt writes:

9. G.C. Nerlich, *Values and Valuing: Speculations on the Ethical Life of Persons*, (Oxford, Clarendon Press, 1989), p. 3.

> Besides wanting and choosing and being moved *to do* this or that, men may also want to have (or not to have) certain desires and motives. They are capable of wanting to be different, in their preferences and purposes, from what they are. . . . No animal other than man, however, appears to have the capacity for reflective self-evaluation that is manifested in the formation of second-order desires.[10]

While a second-order desire is the desire that one have a first-order desire one currently does not have, it is not necessary that the second-order desire will of course be satisfied. For it may be entertained as an idle wish, like my wishing that I actually desire to run five kilometers everyday. But I may genuinely desire that my desire to run that much every morning be *effective* in moving me actually to do so. That is, I may want this desire to become my *will*. In this case I am said to have a second-order volition, which, for Frankfurt, is "essential to being a person".[11]

An important claim of Frankfurt's is that it is the ability to form second-order volitions, satisfiable or not, that concerns a person's freedom of the will. A person always must be an "entity for whom the freedom of the will is a problem"[12] — that is, a person must be capable of forming second-order volitions. And having freedom of the will — hence having a solution to the problem — consists in having the will one wants, that is having one's second-order volitions satisfied.

It is the idea of the freedom of the will being *problematic* to personhood that speaks for personal self-encounter while experiencing conflict of desires. The human character that consists of a persistent pattern of first-order desires normally resists change. It presents a problem to the person's higher-order desires and to the effort of forming second-order

---

10. H. Frankfurt, "Identification and Wholeheartedness" in F. Schoeman (ed.), *Responsibility, Character and the Emotions*, (Cambridge, Cambridge Univ. Press, 1987), p.7.

11. *Ibid.*, p. 10.

12. *Ibid.*, p. 14.

motivations — that is, to render second-order desires so effective as to transform the basic character in a way recommended by reflective self-evaluation. Since desires of different orders do conflict, persons are characteristically beings engaged in inner struggle, and bent on evolving their own inner structures. An internal dialectical conflict between self-alienation and self-transcendence characterises the evolution of personal life.

Second-order desires, being higher-order normative self-attitudes, are *judgements* upon our desires which move us to first-order actions. These judgements involve retrospective assessment of our actions, satisfactions and emotions — in short, our already formed character. They are thus occasioned by judgements of self-appraisal and by an attitude of self-excelling. Because of higher-order self-attitudes of normatively well-developed kinds, a human subject considers herself, or what she does, an object of *value* for herself, an *être pour soi*, or what is properly a person. It is in acting on second-order desires of a crucial sort that we, as persons, choose our identities, our idealised characters. The object of our crucial second-order desires are those first-order desires with which we identify ourselves in making a decision to act on them. In Frankfurt's words:

> To this extent the person, in making a decision by which he identifies with a desire, *constitutes himself*.[13]

STRONG EVALUATION

To the extent that our crucial second-order desires are reflective and expressive of our normatively chosen self-identities, there is something special about the nature of reflective self-evaluations that underlie the formation of such identity-determinative desires. What makes them crucial is, of course, their constitutive role in shaping our self-identities. But what is special about the underlying self-evaluations is that the self engages in what Charles Taylor calls *strong evaluation*.

---

13. H. Frankfurt, "Identification and Wholeheartedness" in F. Schoeman (ed.), *Responsibility, character and the Emotions*, p. 38.

The evaluation of desires, or desired consummation, can be understood in both a weak and a strong sense. Some second-order desires are *functions* of conflict amongst first-order desires. For example, I may form a second-order desire not to desire to conceal the actual extent of my taxable income, because I believe or fear that if I get caught doing so, it would *result* in the non-satisfaction of my other first-order desire, namely, to keep myself away from the hustles of the income tax department. I set aside one desired alternative, namely concealing the actual extent of my taxable income, only on grounds of its contingent incompatibility with the other, more desired alternative, namely avoiding a legal action upon me. Here I am weighing the two alternatives simply to determine, non-qualitatively, that which is more convenient to me. Someone engaged in this sort of non-qualitative evaluation — non-qualitative because the evaluation does not take into consideration the intrinsic qualitative character of the desired actions — is, according to Taylor "a simple weigher of alternatives"[14], or a weak evaluator.

There may, on the other hand, be second-order desires to act, or to desist from acting, on certain first-order desires, not because doing, or not doing, so is grounded simply on matters of convenience, or because of contingent incompatibility of one desire with another, more desired, alternative; but because the desires under evaluation are classified by the agent in such qualitative categories as higher or lower, virtuous or vicious, noble or base. The desires are judged, according to Taylor,

> as belonging to qualitatively different modes of life, fragmented or integrated, alienated or free, saintly or merely human, courageous or pusillanimous, and so on.[15]

Thus, what makes my second-order desire to desist from concealing the actual taxable amount of my earnings a matter

---

14. C. Taylor, "Responsibility for Self" in A. Rorty (ed.), *op. cit.*, p. 287.

15. *Ibid.*, p. 282.

of weak evaluation is that I do not excercise my decision to reveal, rather than conceal, my total earnings out of my conviction that tax evasion is bad and unbecoming of a good citizen's life. Rather, my decision is motivated by the non-qualitative reflection that deciding otherwise would result in my being subjected to legal harassment. The desirability of non-concealment is defined by me in terms of a calculation of consequences and by the fact that I am more strongly drawn to the second desired alternative than to the first. But it would be an instance of strong evaluation if I eschew tax evasion, not because the consummation of the desire to evade tax is contingently incompatible with the desire to remain unharassed by the income tax department, but because I cast the former desire as morally wrong and reflective of a debased character. In so defining the desire, I characterise it *contrastively* in relation to the alternative desire that I decide to act upon. The incompatibility of the eschewed desire with the accepted desire is of non-contingent kind. The rejected desire is rejected because it is considered a base one, and the accepted desire is accepted because it is believed to be ethically desirable.

Contrastive characterisation of desires or motivations is indicative of awareness of, and sensitivity to, the qualitative depth of particular mode of life. As a strong evaluator who defines desires contrastively, I form second-order desires precisely because I am motivated to cast myself as a person of a certain kind, to live a kind of life shaped by the virtues of courage, nobility, integrity, honour, and so on. My evaluative vision draws out for me a preferred mode of life by virtue of qualitative reflection upon the desires and motivations which express and sustain a life of that kind. My motivations or desires matter to me, not so much because of the attraction of their consummations, but in virtue of the quality of the kind of life and the kind of character that these desires properly belong to.

I suppose the foregoing discussion makes it sufficiently understandable why we would be tempted to make strong evaluation an essential characteristic of a person. Taylor summarises the reason for regarding persons as essentially strong evaluators:

> For any being who was incapable of evaluating desires (as my dog, e.g., is incapable), or who could only evaluate as a simple weigher, would lack the depth to be a potential interlocutor, a potential partner of human communion, be it as friend, lover, confidant, or whatever. And we cannot see one who could not enter into any of these relations as a normal human subject.[16]

V

Wanting as Valuing: Personal Ascent to Freedom

DESIRING AND VALUING

There is no gainsaying the fact that human freedom does not consist merely in our being able to do what we desire to do, or whatever pleases us to do. Only a very naïve or impoverished thought about freedom would uphold such a puerile view. Indeed, such a view would blantantly betray the nature of a person who is truly free. I may act on a desire, say the desire to conspire against you, and so do what I want, namely go on slandering you, and yet feel the desire alien and hostile. The alienation and hostility of the desire may be to my preferred self-identity, to my idealised personal self-image. I would then feel that, contrary to my being free to do as I desired to do, I am actually encumbered with a passion which keeps me in 'bondage' — which impedes my freedom to be the kind of person I want to be.

This problem of freedom, or of unfreedom, is a problem of consistency or conflict between values and desires. If I feel that the desire upon which I act is alien and hostile, it means that I disvalue the desire and disapprove of acting on it. My being motivated by such a desire to do something is likely to be most worrisome to me. Certainly this is not a very uncommon

16. C. Taylor, "Responsibility for Self" in A. Rorty (ed.), *op. cit.*, p. 289.

human predicament, and the struggle to get over it by virtue of attaining an ideal consistency between what one values and what one desires is a prominent mark of personhood.

The discrepancy between desiring and valuing may be of the radical and rare kind, in which what one desires to do is not *at all* valued, held to be good or worthwhile, such as the impulsive and transient desire of a mother to drown her own baby in the bathwater, or the desire of the runner-up player in a game of tennis to smash the face of the champion with the racket. And there may be desires of a more persistent and pervasive kind, more long-standing and dispositional variety, which diverge less radically from what one values, and the strength of which does not properly reflect the degree to which one values the object of such a desire. An example of this variety would be the desire to have non-vegetarian meals, which one values for the taste and the nourishing quality, but still does not value the desire so whole-heartedly as to have no qualms about it whatsoever. For one might sincerely value a vegetarian diet more than a non-vegetarian one on the ground of one's belief that the latter risks unwholesome increase in the cholesterol level. So the desire for non-vegetarian meals contains a motivational strength that exceeds the extent to which the desire is considered worth-satisfying.

There are certain other desires which are of less motivational strength in relation to the degree to which the object of the desire is valued. Here the motivational strength of the desire falls short of the higher evaluative rating of the desired act or object, such that even though the agent believes the action or object to be of great worth, and she is also motivated to attain it, yet she is unable to be fully spontaneous in pursuing it. She seems to need to make some effort to attain the desired goal. Think, for example, the case of regular physical exercise which one values most because one values a healthy life, but yet one may have to give a fillip to one's desire to get up early in the morning and do the excercises. Or think of a man who goes to cast his vote on the election day somewhat half-heartedly, even though he believes, and hence assigns a high value to the fact, that a good citizen must excercise his franchise.

MOTIVATIONAL AND EVALUATIONAL SYSTEMS

Given that what one desires most strongly is not necessarily what one most values, there is a clear sense in which wanting *as* desiring differs from wanting *as* valuing. Indeed, it can safely be asserted that wanting as desiring belongs to one 'system' and wanting as valuing belongs to another, such that while the two systems may coincide — that is, what one desires to do **is** *also* what one really values, and the motivational strength of the desire is roughly commensurate with the degree to which the object of the desire is valued — the systems may also run in relative independece from one another. And it is the lack of proper coordination between the two systems that constitutes a critical problem of personhood. For to the extent the systems are not harmonised, the person has a conflict to resolve, so that the spontaneity of personal freedom can be realised.

A 'systematic' division of the human self of this kind has been made by Gary Watson in the course of developing a theory of human freedom. Watson construes the problem of free action as a problem that arises both because what one desires may not be what one values, and because what one most values may not be what one is finally moved to attain. He believes that this distinction between desiring and valuing, or what I might describe as wanting-as-desiring and wanting-as-valuing, is not drawn to specify the different contents of wanting-as-desiring and wanting-as-valuing. "The distinction has rather to do with the *source* of the want or with its role in the total 'system' of the agent's desires and ends. It has to do with why the agent wants what he does."[17] And the two systems are, in Watson's own terminology, the *valuational* system, or the system of wanting-as-valuing, and the *motivational* system, or the system of wanting-as-desiring.

---

17. G. Watson, "Free Agency" in G. Watson (ed.), *Free will* (Oxford, Oxford Univ. Press, 1982). p, 102.

While the motivational system of an agent is identified by identifying what motivates or moves her to action, the valuational system consists in a set of her all-things-considered judgements of the form: "the thing for me to do in these circumstances is X". Watson then goes on to identify the problem of freedom of action, and to state what free agency consists in:

> The broblem is that there are motivational factors other than valuational ones. The free agent has the capacity to translate his values into action; his actions flow from his evaluational system.[18]

The role of the valuational system in the life of person is pivotal in that the system constitutes the person's *point of view* from which she judges the world and thereby judges her own place in the world. The system difines her *Weltanschauung* and provides the parameters in terms of which she plays the role of a strong evaluator. It is also inconceivable that one dissociates oneself from one's evaluational system altogether without forfeiting all normative standpoints (that is, all ends and principles) and therewith one's identity as a person. Watson therefore reiterates the centrality of the evaluational system in a person as a free agent:

> One can dissociate oneself from one set of ends and principles only from the standpoint of another such set that one does not disclaim.[19]

If the full resources of our evaluational system are what enter into the constitution of us as normal human agents, then the sense in which we are free, and therefore responsible, agents is that these resources are *available* to us for proper use in the governance of our desires and actions, irrespectives of whether we actually do so or not. We are, or think we are, at liberty to exercise evaluational judgements, and to make such judgements effective in controlling our first-order desires and actions. Our second-order volitions are gounded in, and sustained by, our evaluational systems. On the other hand, our unfreedom is a

18. G. Watson, "Free Agency" in G. Watson (ed.), *Free will*, p. 106.

19. *Ibid*.

matter of our being unduly constrained, inhibited, interfered with, by something which prevents us from the effective exercise of evaluational judgements.

It would now be evident why the victims of hypnosis, coercion, and kleptomania are unfree in being motivated to do what they do. What explains the unfreedom of any compulsive behaviour is that the behaviour is a response to a desire that expresses itself independently of the agent's evaluational judgements. Here the agent is either in situations that inhibit her ability to make evaluational judgements at all, or she is in the grip of desires so strong as to compel her to do what she does, whether she values the action or not.

BRAVE NEW WORLD CITIZENS

Apart from cases of psychological compulsion as instances of unfreedom, there is the interesting case of the imaginary citizens of Aldous Huxley's *Brave New World*, who are so controlled by certain human agents and institutions as to be left with no option but to have the beliefs, choices and values they actually have. Their entire apparatus of congnitive and evaluative faculties is a result of psychological conditioning, even though they do have evaluational systems as distinct from motivational systems, and the ability to make evaluational judgements with which they identify themselves. Apparently, then, the condition of free agency as defined by Watson can be satisfied by the envisioned citizens of the Brave New World. But surely they are *not* free agents, because their cognitions, volitions and evaluations are manipulated in a crucial way. And the impairment caused to them severely affects the normal plasticity of self-reflection and reflective comprehension of theoretical ideas and values.

Citizens of the Brave New World have no control over their identification with the evaluational selves in that they are *caused* to identify with such selves, or their evaluational systems, by conditions over which they have no control. They are not in a position to stand back their attachments and decisions, and to reconsider these in view of a fuller knowledge of their causes and influences. In a later article Watson articulates the reasons for which the subjects in the Brave New World are unfree:

> The subjects in the Brave New World cases lack freedom not because their decisions can be deterministically explained, nor because they are caused by human agents, but because their evaluational and volitional and cognitive faculties have been impaired in certain ways. The crucial thing about their situation is that they are incapable of effectively envisaging or seeing the significance of certain alternatives, of reflecting on themselves and on the origins of their motivations, of comprehending or responding to relevant theoretical and evaluational critieria.[20]

VI

The Spectrum of Moral Personhood

FREEDOM AS A PREROGATIVE

In the preceding section freedom has been defined in terms of the actualisation of a life in which a person's motivational system is governed by her evaluational system, and her evaluational, volitional and cognitive faculties are unimpaired — meaning thereby that she is sufficiently capable of standing back from her inclinations and decisions in order to reassess what she desires and chooses to do in the light of further and richer knowledge of the sources or causes of the indignations and decisions. In this view, freedom is the supreme feature of a human person's being a *centre of significance*, an embodiment of value, and at best a self-evaluating being. For it is in virtue of the ability to be free, in this sense, the ability to motivate herself to live her life in conformity with her evaluational system, that she, as a human subject, transcends the level of a brute animal's life.

In being able to attain freedom *towards* the realisation of higher values, the human agent also succeeds in attaining freedom *from* these desires and appetites which tend to seek

20. G. Watson, "Free Action and Free will", *Mind* 96, p. 12.

satisfaction independently of the subject's evaluative endorsement. If humans are considered 'higher' animals, the sense in which they are so considered is not so much that they are more sophisticated than the 'lower' animals, as that humans have the unique ability to *rise* above the gross animal level. It is *this* sense of 'higher' that is relevant to the sense in which humans cherish values, and judge their own lives in terms of worth. Only then do they become properly persons.

Freedom is then a prerogative of persons. It is the driving spirit of personal excellence. Most of all, it paves the path of moral perfectibility. It is her that the intimacy of the relation between human freedom and human morality can be sensed. This is the issue of concern in the discussion of this section.

That personal self-excelling requires that a person have an evaluational system which is both rich and deep in content, and with which the person identifies herself, is by now not a fact that can be gainsaid. The person's motivational system surely needs to be controlled by her evaluational system. Or, as the traditional proverbial saying goes, one's reason has to control one's passion. But what must be stressed is the fact that a person's evaluational system at any particular period of time need not be, and is generally not, the same as the evaluational system she espouses at another time, whether earlier or later. The evaluational system can evolve and even undergo drastic change depending upon the person's exposure to new values, different circumstances and knowledge of informations in course of life, all filtered through critical self-reflection. The prevailing wisdom of a culture is always a great source from which a person would draw its values provided she is rightly responsive to the positive content of that culture.

A SYSTEMIC PARALLELISM

It can be hypothesised that there is a spectrum of moral personhood that represents qualitatively different levels of evaluational systems —that is, evaluational systems of different degrees of depth or profundity in the qualitative scale of value

– *vis-à-vis* motivational systems with correspondingly differrent levels of refinement and control of passions and appetites, inclinations and weaknesses. We can describe the spectrum as having a 'lower' side and as having a 'higher' side, both the sides being polar opposites of one another, like the lower end and the upper end of a vertical axis. The lower side begins with the 'lowest' pair of parallels, which consists of an evaluational system of minimum depth coupled with a motivational system of passions and inclinations that are minimally refined or controlled by the corresponding evaluational system of minimal depth. The higher side ends with the 'highest' pair of parallels, namely an evaluational system consisting of the deepest values, and a corresponding motivational system containing the least amount, or none at all, of any intransigent or resilient passions.

Evidently this sort of pairing of evaluational and motivational systems along a spectrum with lower and higher ends is more a heuristic device than a veridical representation of what is actually the case in the moral psychology of human persons. However, the spectrum-model is pertinent for its explanatory value. It at least would help explain, as I hope to show, two important points: (a) the attainment of moral personhood is a matter of degree; and (b) moral striving, as it is aimed at perfect moral personhood, is not just rational, but spiritual.

GRADES OF MORAL PERSONALITY

Since appetites and passions characterise human nature at its most primary level, they form the dominant part of a human creature's motivational system. To the extent that we humans are a biological species, we are fundamentally appetitively and passionately disposed beings. And it is intrinsic to the appetites and passions that they engender (or consist in) desires which persist and motivate us to a life of instinctual satisfaction – a non-rational and hence non-valuational life altogether. Our innocent infancy testifies to this claim, much as our culpable debauchery testisfies to the same claim in another way.

As the innocent child gradually matures through cognitive

and other developments, the light of reason flickers, so to speak, and, with that, a rudimentary evaluational system gets a grip in her psyche. It is at this juncture that the child begins to have an inchoate experience of what might be called a *self-encounter*, that is an encounter between her biologically endowed motivational system and her cognitively and culturally acquired evaluational system. From then on begins for her a life of conflict between desiring and valuing, between wanting-as-desiring and wanting-as-valuing. Her moral life becomes a biographical narrative of the various ways in which she tries to resolve the perpetual conflict — a narrative of her successes and failures in harmonising the two systems or in controlling her motivations by her evaluative stance towards her own life.

While the preceding paragraph appears to present an empirical account in moral-developmental psychology, this is not what I really intend to present. It is enough if what has been speculatively said here is roughly true of the structure of actual moral-psychological development. And I believe the structural account is couched in sufficiently broad terms to secure conformity to the facts of the matter.

Granted the plausibility of the structural account, it can now be asserted that the 'lowest-level' pair of parallels between the evaluational system and the motivational system is instantiated by the case of the child who just enters the cognitive-cum-cultural domain of value-awareness (the prodigious child excepted, of course), and just begins to experience, howsoever inchoately, the confrontation between the acquired value-awareness and the already given impulses that demand immediate satisfaction. It is at this level that the human child makes her maiden transition to moral personhood. An inarticulate moral self emerges as the regulative agent of her desires and actions and the direction of her life.

The lowest-level parallelism between the evaluational system and the motivational system exemplified in such a child's inner life does not imply that the seriousness of the confrontation here is the least. Rather, the criterion of seriousness is inappropriate here. The child's cognitive-evaluational system is not rich enough to be of proper regulative use; nor is she committed to the system in a sufficiently serious way. Indeed, the confrontation fails to gather adequate momentum so as to make any substantive morality out of it. If it gets the status of a moral conflict, the status is more or less gratuitous. That such a child's so-called moral net is knitted with wide holes is borne out by the fact that, when confronted with the option of either satisfying a desire or foregoing the desired consummation for the sake of something morally worth-achieving, children often give into the desire. This is not surprising, nor is it terribly worrisome.

What **is** terribly worrisome is the proclivity of mature humans towards the consummation of desires in disregard of any evaluation of the object of desire, or because of akratic surrender to the seductiveness of the desired consummation. For what looms large in such ungoverned proclivities is either an ignominous regression to crass immaturity, or an appalling discomfiture in the endeavour to realise the ideals of personhood. Both are seriously counteractive to moral personhood.

The confrontation between the two systems of evaluation and motivation gathers the momentum of a significant moral conflict only when a mature agent takes the event of self-encounter quite seriously — that is, when the agent experiences a conflict between her desire and her value as a *decisive* moment in the determination of what sort of person she is going to be. This means that the agent's evaluational system has to be much richer and deeper than a naïve one. It will have to include a higher-order consciousness of the *moral* significance of the system itself, which is the significance of the role of the system in articulating a picture of the person the agent identifies herself with.

QUALITATIVE REFINEMENT

In a plain sense, it can be held that a human agent attains moral personhood *to the extent* she actually succeeds in evaluatively controlling her motivational system and also in refining the contents of that system. Evaluative refinement of motivational forces or elements is quite important in this regard bacause no real moral progress can be made without a measure of drastic changes in such forces. Certain desires and inclinations are such as directly to obstruct the internalisation of moral values. Indeed, much traditional moral and religious thought views some desires as a kind of compulsion from which human beings requires deliverance. While Freudianism limits the possibility of such deliverance to sublimation of desires, others, such as Buddhism, advocate the more austere requirement of total renunciation of all desires. In any case, the general truth about the immorality of some desires, or desires at all, is that moral constraint is largely a constraint of some desires, or desires as such.

If we take into consideration Buddhist morality and its complete denunciation of desire, we would face a unique theory of moral personhood, according to which the idealised moral (or religious) person, while having an evaluational system consisting of extraordinarily rich and deep ideas and values, would have to have a motivational system which contains no desires at all. The motivational system would be far too radically refined, and drastically overhauled, under the aegis of the Four Noble Truths, the Eightfold Path, etc., which make up the corresponding evaluational system. But a vital question necessarily arises here: what would be the positive content of a Buddhist motivational system as a parallel to a Buddhist evaluational system? What kind of motivational content would characterise the psyche of a person who is perpetually in a state of complete desirelessness? Certainly this question is of paramount importance to a theory of moral freedom, as well as to moral personhood.

We may return to our discussion of the less austere kind of moral personhood, which does not disallow the inclusion of any desires but disallows some on moral-evaluative grounds. For a good start, let's go through a passage, quoted by Robert

Grant from George Orwell's *A Road to Wigan Pier*:

> I am a degenerate modern semi-intellectual who would die if I did not get my early morning cup of tea and my *New Statesman* every Friday. Clearly I do not, in a sense, 'want' to return to a simpler, harder, probably agricultural way of life. In the same sense I don't want to pay my debts, to take enough exercise, to be faithful to my wife, etc. But in another and more permanent sense I do want these things, and perhaps in the same sense I want a civilisation in which 'progress' is not definable as making the world safe for little fat men.[21]

Orwell's confessional remark is a fine illustration of a fairly mature-level parallelism between an evaluational system and a motivational system. It indicates a tension in him between the two systems, between wanting the consummation of certain desires for sheer pleasure, and wanting, in a 'more permanent sense', to lead another kind of life that would cast him as a socially responsible, temperate, sincere person — a virtuous person in short. It is against the unvalued life of selfishness, irresponsibility and unrestrained hedonism that Orwell wants to forge a virtuous life for himself.

What this higher-order, 'more permanent' want is intended to do is to cleanse the motivational system of denigrated desires, and thereby to sow the seeds of virtuous dispositions, so to speak. Thus the evaluational system provides new motivational input, so that the output becomes the actual life of person transfigured in the system. If freshly programmes the motivational system in order that the person develops herself in accordance with a new motivational dynamism. And once the evaluationally transfigured life is motivationally actualised, the two systems attain the state of equilibrium in relation to one another.

---

21. R.D.A. Grant, "Freedom from What?" in Anderson and Kaplan (eds.). *Morality and Religion in Liberal Democratic Societies*, (New York, Paragon House, 1991), p. 21.

VII

The Motivational Dynamism of Moral Personhood

FROM EVALUATION TO IDENTIFICATION

I have talked, in schematic language, about cleansing the motivational system of unvalued desires, reprogramming it with the seeds of an evaluationally transfigured life, and actualising that life through the impact of a new motivational dynamism — a dynamism that facilitates the sprouting forth of the new seeds of moral personhood. What is it, as the question may pertinently be raised, that genuinely and centrally lends dynamism to the freshly programmed motivational system? What, in other words, animates the agent's efficacious striving for progressive levels of moral personhood?

This question is important in view of the undeniable fact that merely judging that something is good or valuable has no invariable connection with being actually motivated to realise the good or value. Surely the agent has to identify with the evaluational judgement in order to get any motivational mileage from it. But if identification is what underpins efficacious motivational dynamism, it needs to be analysed in view of its special role as a sufficient condition of actual moral endeavour — that is, the speciality of identification as that which triggers off moral motivation. The identification has to be of a particular character which is uniquely relevant to moral motivation.

IDENTIFICATION, SPIRITUALITY AND SELFLESSNESS

I claim that the morally relevant type of identification is characterised by *spirituality*. In identifying with an evaluational judgement which bears on moral personhood, an agent is not just emotionally attached to the judgement or value, but is in *spiritual accord* with the judgement or value. Any ascent in the heirarchy of moral personhood is not just an evidence of the agent's being habituated to a worthwhile mode of life, but a testimony to a gradual *regeneration of personal being*, of personhood itself. Moral uplift is spiritual uplift.

The reason why unfailing moral personhood truly depends upon spiritual sustenance is, principally, the absolute and unconditional requirement of *transcendence of the ego*, or freedom from ego-centricity. Ego-centricity, or selfishness, is the ultimate obstacle to, and hence its overcoming is the litmus test of, moral personhood. When any lower-order desire is the target of morally relevant higher-order desire, or of strong evaluation, the higher-order attitude aims at the target with a view to undercutting the ego-centric support that sustains the target desire. To revert to the Orwell example cited in the preceding section, the life of first-order desires that Orwell does not really want to identify with is a target of higher-order self-attitude precisely because that kind of life feeds on egoistic gratifications. That life is discredited because egoism or selfishness, in which that life is anchored, is denigrated.

Transcending one's ego, or overcoming selfishness, demands a peculiar kind of inner personal transmutation, and it is extremely difficult to articulate its peculiarity. It is not, as I have already said, like becoming accustomed to a new trait of character, developed by following mechanically a set of practical rules. Nor is it like a shift in psychological attitude manipulatively brought about by brainwashing. For either of these fails to be genuinely an inner transformation at the deeply personal level. Indeed, no positive empirical characterisation of the process or experience of ego-transcendence seems to be possible. That is why it appears more apposite to resort to a non-empirical characterisation of transcendence, namely *spiritual* transcendence. The practice or attempt of attaining a life of moral values, inasmuch as this is a life beyond selfishness, is a practice in spirituality.

I therefore think that moral striving consists in a life whose motivational system derives its dynamism from nowhere else but the moral agent's spiritual exercise. Moral motivation is, ultimately, spiritual motivation. It is only when the motivation is spiritual that the agent acts with the moral self, and the moral self is that spiritual standpoint which positions the agent in a direction diametrically against the standpoint of selfishness. In other words, moral agency at its best attains a selfhood whose essence is *selflessness*.

What I am labouring to drive home is the point that the normative judgements of practical reason, which provide substantive content to one's moral-evaluational system, do not automatically motivate the agent towards the actualisation of moral personhood. For there still is a *hiatus* between accepting, even whole-heartedly, the verdict of practical reason as a moral imperative, and practically securing the required innner transformation that moral personhood genuinely consists in. While this hiatus has to be crossed over, the evaluational resources of practical reason alone do not make that possible. Of course the agent has to identify with the evaluational judgements of practical reason for these to be motivationally efficacious. But such an identification would still be inconsequential unless the state or attitude of identification assumes the distinctive role of a spiritual engagement. It is only when the agent is spiritually engaged with the values, which she accepts because she wants her life to conform to the ideals of moral personhood, that her identification with these values involves into her edification.

What transpires from the above account of the sequence from evaluation to edification *via* the intermediary of identification is that reason or judgement, unaided by the endeavour of spirituality, does not *eo ipso* set the agent on the path of moral personhood. For to be actually set on this path is, for the agent, to have already drawn herself away from the mire of ego-centricity, whatsoever may be the extent of reaching beyond the ego. It means that she would have had buttressed her evaluational stance with the unique urge of spiritual self-excelling. More importantly, her motivational system would have had an input — the unique spiritual urge — which is not intrinsic to her evaluational system.

A NON-RATIONAL INGREDIENT

The crucial upshot of the foregoing discussion, which I wish to proclaim expressly, is that the unique spiritual input to the motivational system of a moral agent, which I have claimed to be extrinsic to the agent's evaluational system, is extrinsic to rationally itself. The spiritual urge of ego-transcendence, of self-transmutation into selflessness, is of course not a natural urge of passion: but nor is it an urge of reason. Indeed, while this urge is non-natural or non-empirical, it is non-rational as well. It is *sui generis*, and it forms the ultimate determinant of moral motivation and of moral personhood.

Given the non-natural and non-rational ingredient of moral personhood, it would follow that such a theory of moral personhood is at once different from empiricism and rationalism. It differs from rationalism to the extent that, though reason inevitably engenders evaluational insights, what ultimately conduces to the practical embodiment of moral values is something non-rational in itself. In regard of this latter claim, this position differs significantly from the Platonic theory according to which reason itself, in the normative or practical sense of reason, motivates the agent towards leading a moral life.

In being the *sine qua non* of an authentic moral life, the uniqueness of spiritual motivation or endeavour is also a testimony to the uniqueness of human persons. The spiritual possibility within us bespeaks of the possibility of purging our motivational system of all desires and other ego-centric predilections — in the way the Buddhists have talked about. Once the motivational system is so purified, it may then draw all its dynamism from the spiritual itself, and yet still keep the person intact as a moral agent. In a most serious sense, moral personhood as a spiritual quest necessarily points towards an end as projected by Buddhism. At that sublime end, morality meets religion.

2

What is it to be a Moral Agent

R.C. Pradhan

THIS article seeks to address the question raised in this volume and highlighted especially in Bijoy Boruah's article,[1] namely: What is it that constitutes a moral person or agent? My task is to delineate certain issues already raised in Boruah's article and to provide a metaphysical framework[2] for understanding the nature of the moral agent. For the present purpose, I will use 'moral agent' and 'moral person' interchangeably for the reason that it is only moral persons who are moral agents. I do not take persons as such as moral agents because only a morally committed person could be a moral agent.

My task here is twofold: first, I will show that moral agents have moral commitments which define their moral personhood, and second, I will argue that mere second-order desires are not enough to define a moral agent: the moral agent must partake of higher ideals and commitments which qualify her to be a moral person.

---

1. See Bijoy H. Boruah's article in this volume. It presents a theory of moral personhood. His main contention is that moral personhood aims at the transcendence of ego-centricity. I have argued for a similar thesis in my paper.

2. I believe that the moral agent is the same as the moral person. The moral persons enjoy the same metaphysical status as the moral agents in our conceptual scheme.

Moral agency and moral commitments

There is an irreducible concept of moral agency which is presupposed by our valuational activities. The moral agent is the source of the moral actions which involve an element of moral valuation. That is the reason why the moral agent is associated with a whole gamut of moral valuation, motivation and moral commitment. The moral agent can therefore be defined as one who is morally committed and thus strongly morally motivated.[3] The ideas of moral motivation and self-intervention[4] have been the cornerstone of much of moral psychology that has taken the moral self seriously.

The moral self is the most important concept to be analysed in connection with the notion of moral agency. It is the moral self that is involved in all cases of moral agency. So the basic question is: Who is the moral agent? The answer of course is: the self that acts in all cases of moral actions is the moral agent. Here we need clarification of the concept of moral actions. These actions, like all actions, are undertaken by an agent and there is a definite plan underlying them since they are intentional actions. Thus moral actions are in continuation of the human actions in general which are embedded in the human self, the human agent. Agency defines all human actions, since the actor or doer is the primary source of all intentional actions. Carlos J. Moya has to say this about agency: What is important about agency is what connects it with such notions as will and freedom.[5] What is suggested here is the fact that the agent wills the actions and thus intentionally executes them. It is the agent which executes the actions in order to fulfil a goal or purpose. In this sense, the intentional actions are free and hence morally significant.

---

3. Cf. William P. Alston, "Self-Intervention and the Structure of Motivation" in *The Self*, ed. Theodore Mischel, (Basil Blackwell, Oxford, 1977), pp. 65-102.

4. *Ibid.*

5. Carlos J. Moya, *The Philosophy of Action: An Introduction*, (The Polity Press, Cambridge, 1990), p. 10.

However, the moral actions are not any actions undertaken with a purpose. They have to be undertaken with a serious moral purpose. That is, the moral actions are everything the actions are plus the moral motivation and commitment. These committed sorts of actions bear the seriousness of the moral self that fulfils certain moral obligations in undertaking the moral actions. For example, the moral agent *A* seeks to fulfil the moral obligation *O* by doing the action *C*. In this action the agent *A* is committed to fulfilling the moral obligation *O* by choosing to perform the action *C*, e.g., sacrificing herself for the welfare of humanity. The action of sacrificing oneself needs a high moral motivation and commitment. Only a morally serious agent will do this. Here one can notice that the agent is under no compulsion to do so, though she is aware that she has a duty towards humanity. This sense of duty is so high that the agent cannot fail to lay down her life for the sake of the welfare humanity.

Moral motivation of the above sort are rare but not humanly impossible. Such cases of moral actions are the ideal cases in the history of mankind. There are, however, different degrees of moral motivation which manifest in various kinds of moral actions. Some moral actions like a mother's going hungry for the sake of the child, or a friend's jumping into water for rescuing a friend are cases of moral actions that require a high degree of seriousness. One can say that these actions are more spontaneous than planned and so they are not motivated at all. But one must understand the whole moral personality of the agent in order to assess her morally courageous behaviour. It could not be the case that the agent did the action without realising the consequences or not knowing that her life is at stake. All that she has done is that she has obeyed the dictates of her inner being which consists in a high degree of moral selflessness. Alston, in depicting the serious character of moral motivation, says the following:

> A still higher degree of cognitive sophistication is involved where the self-concept or one's evaluation of oneself figure in the objects

> of one's W's and B's; as when one has a desire for one's own self-esteem or self-approval, and an aversion to one's own self-rejection or self-disapproval.[6]

The moral agent is thus supposed to be aware of herself and her own worth in undertaking an action. She is evaluating herself in terms of the value that accrues to her self in terms of the actions and its consequences.

Moral motivations thus have both cognitive and conative elements that result in what we have called the moral commitments. The cognitive awareness of the nature of the values involved in the moral actions and the conative espousal of the values define the moral commitment the agent makes to herself. A moral commitment is a motivation to do a certain action under all circumstances. The following is the way a moral commitment could be defined:

> (M) The moral commitment consists in choosing a moral principle or value and reflecting it in one's actions without bothering about the consequences.

That is to say, a moral commitment follows from the sense of moral values or principles involved in an action. The moral agent expresses her moral commitment by steadfastly doing the moral action out of a sense of moral obligation. She would not have done the action if it were not for fulfilling the moral obligation which comes out of her moral sense or the sense of values. The moral sense is reflected in the values one pursues and the principles one adopts in one's actions.

Following Alston,[7] we can make a distinction between Lower Level Motives and Higher Level Motives in moral actions. The Lower Level Motives reflect a lower degree of moral seriousness in the sense that one is bogged down in one's petty desires and motives. For example, the desire to serve one's group or clan is a lower moral motive than the motive to serve all

---

6. Alston, *op. cit.*, p. 75.
7. *Ibid.*

irrespective of caste, creed and religion. The latter motive generates the moral commitment to human values like brotherhood, peace and friendship among all. But the former, that is,the lower moral motivation generates at some level or other the disvalue of hatred, conflict and disharmony among groups and communities. In this sense we can say there are different levels of moral motivation depending on what we pursue as our values. The higher we ascend the moral hierarchy the more moral seriousness we encounter and the higher moral values we stumble upon. Thus, we have to recognise the fact that moral commitments are commensurate with our moral seriousness and moral motivation.

The moral agents are distinguishable from ordinary human agents by the fact that the former, not the latter, are committed to certain moral goals and standards. Because of this commitment, the moral agents are found to be endowed with serious motivation. In the absence of this commitment, the agent is supposed to be non-serious and hence non-moral. The moral goals are generally set by the society and, more often than not, are enforced by the society. But this sort of social morality cannot be better than the Nietzschean herd-morality which lacks ethical seriousness. The moral agent here is under no commitment to fulfil the moral goal except under the fear of public disapproval. That is why it has been emphasised by the moral philosophers that the individual moral agent herself must be involved in the acts of moral choice and be autonomous so far as the moral actions are concerned. The moral autonomy enjoyed by the moral agent must thus pave the way for moral progress that is not dependent on the accepted moral practices of the society. The moral genius must be allowed to set a new moral standard unheard of so far. This alone explains how a Buddha or a Christ or a Gandhi is possible as a moral genius. A moral genius has a higher level of reflective awareness and so has moral sensibility that knows no conventional bounds. Nevertheless, the moral genius does not differ from a rational morally committed person. Generalising this trait of moral seriousness to all moral agents, Moya claims:

> The level of reflection, norm following and commitment distinguishes human agents from the higher non-human animals. This level allows agents to filter the influence of desires on their actions and to act in a way that can be autonomous as to the relative strength of desires.[8]

If this is true of any normal human agent, then it is more so of the moral agents who are possessed of a high sense of moral commitment. The moral agent is a determined moral actor known for her utmost moral commitment.

The moral will and the moral reasons

The moral agent is a rational agent in the sense that the moral commitments we ascribe to her are prompted by her moral will. The will is that feature of a moral agent that gives the necessary standards to distinguish between the higher and the lower moral reasons. The moral will, as Kant[9] has said, is the autonomous source of all morality and therefore it alone matters in all matters of ethical concern. The moral will carries the entire burden of moral freedom enjoyed by the moral agent. The moral will thus occupies a significant place in any account of moral agency and moral commitment.

The moral reasons have a logical connection with the moral will in the sense that the moral will issues in the offering of reasons for moral actions. We can define a moral reason in the following way:

> (R) The reason *R* is a moral reason for the action *C* if and only if *R* explains and constitutes *C* as a moral action.

That is to say, *R* as moral reason is sufficient enough to constitute the moral action *C*. For example, the moral action of self-sacrifice for the sake of humanity can be explained by the

8. Moya, *op. cit.*, p. 169.

9. See Lewis White Beck, *A Commentary on Kant's Critique of Practical Reason*, (The University of Chicago Press, Chicago and London, 1960), chapter XI.

moral reason of saving mankind from a certain moral catastrophe. Here the moral reason is part of the action of sacrificing oneself. In this sense the moral reasons are not the causes of the moral actions but are rather the normative bases of the moral actions. Thus the moral will which offers these reasons is already involved in the moral actions.

Moral reasons have to be objective and universal in the sense that they can hold good as reasons not only for me but also for everybody in my situation. That is, the agent must be able to offer these reasons as reasons in all similar situations. The situation which demands sacrifice in the case of Gandhi will demand similar sacrifice on the part of, say, Martin Luther King Jr., the Black crusader against injustice and violation of human rights. Reasons do not change when the individual agents change. The human moral will remains more or less the same even if there are changes in the way the moral agent expresses them. Therefore there is an element of impersonality about moral reasons and the moral will. However, it must be conceded to Thomas Nagel that there is a peculiarly personal element in any set of moral reasons. Nagel writes:

> The problem is to discover the form which reasons for action take, and whether it can be described from no particular point of view. The method is to begin with reasons that appear to obtain from my point of view and those of other individuals, and ask what the best perspectiveless account of those reasons is. As in other domains, we begin from our position inside the world and try to transcend it by regarding what we find here as a sample of the whole.[10]

Thus, there is no escape from the fact that we must begin with the reasons the individual agents have to offer but at the same time we have to transcend our personal perspectives to arrive at the agent-neutral reasons. The agent-neutral reasons make the moral actions more serious than the agent-relative reasons.

The agent-neutral reasons have an edge over the agent-

10. Thomas Nagel, *The View from Nowhere*, (Oxford University Press, New York and Oxford, 1986), p. 141.

relative reasons for the following reasons: first, the agent-relative reasons are narrower than the agent-neutral reasons in the sense that these reasons do not go beyond the subjective considerations of the individual agents; secondly, the agent-neutral reasons are the universal moral reasons that are dictated by the moral will. The moral will is the ultimate source of the reasons and therefore has to be taken as the most fundamental moral universal. Nagel's dilemma in reconciling the personal reasons with the universal reasons must be resolved by taking into consideration the fact that our moral reasoning transcends the limits of the personal reasons for explaining the moral actions. As Kant has shown, the moral reasons have to rise above the subjective level and merge into an objective domain of the practical reason.

The subjective reasons have a built-in drawback about them in the sense that they do not reveal their non-moral character till we find their real worth in terms of their constituting a moral action. For example, an ideologically committed terrorist might justify the terrorist activities in terms of an ideology and thus appear to be very rational. But in actuality the terrorist violates every norm of human dignity and goes against the very human existence. This makes his or her reasons for actions irrational and so immoral. The subjective reasons have nothing to offer except pseudo-reasons for actions. Therefore, a non-subjective universal reason is bound to be appealed to for the sake of explaining the moral actions.

The moral agents have the option of committing themselves to higher moral reasons in the sense that they may appeal to higher moral values than peculiar to a given group or organisation. Humanity is the highest value for the moral agent so far as the human actions and reasons are concerned. In that sense any reason that goes against the human dignity and human existence has to be deemed as lower. Hence ideologies, cults and the so-called group moral codes must be viewed as lower in comparison to the highest human values and reasons.

Moral reasons are the pro-attitudes[11] that provide rational clues to the moral actions. In that sense, the moral reasons are the rationalising principles that explain how a moral action takes place. Therefore, we can say that the moral reasons are the normative elements associated with the moral actions. Normativity of the moral actions depends upon what the principles or reasons are underlying the human actions. If the reason is overtly given as the main principle of action, it goes without saying that the moral actions are constituted out and out by the moral norms underlying them. The moral reason is a kind of commitment to a moral norm in the sense that unless the moral norm is accepted, the agent cannot execute the action. The agent therefore has the idea that the principle or norm must be the bedrock of the moral actions.

The moral reasons are such that the agent has the choice of opting for them or not opting for them. The choice depends entirely on her moral motivation and commitment. A less morally committed person may not offer a reason which the more committed person offers. For example, two agents, *B* and *C*, go for acquiring knowledge but for different reasons. The agent *B* acquires knowledge to amass wealth whereas *C* does the same for the sake of knowledge itself. Here *B*'s reasons are shallow and pragmatic, while *C*'s reasons are deep and sublime. Thus, the latter's reasons are more moral than *B*'s reasons. Here the moral agent exercising his option between two types of reasons emerges as moral evaluator[12] who can rise from his personal reasons to impersonal ones and can distinguish between what is lower and what is higher among reasons. The moral evaluator has a sense of deep moral reasons.

The moral agent as a strong evaluator

The idea of strong evaluation has been introduced by Charles

11. See Donald Davidson,"Actions, Reasons and Causes" in *Essays in Actions and Events*, (Clarendon Press, Oxford, 1980). Reprinted, 1985.

12. See Charles Taylor, "What is Human Agency?" in *The Self*, ed. T. Mischel, pp. 103-35.

Taylor in connection with his definition of human agency. He writes:

> To be a strong evaluator is thus to be capable of a reflection which is more articulate. But it is also in an important sense deeper.
>
> A strong evaluator, by which we mean a subject who strongly evaluates desires, goes deeper, because he characterises his motivation at greater depth. To characterise one desire or inclination as worthier, or nobler, or more integrated, etc., than others is to speak of it in terms of the kind of quality of life which it expresses and sustains.[13]

Thus, a strong evaluator, because of her moral commitments, exercises a complete valuational control over her desires and motives. Thus, she has the deep sense of evaluating a desire as worthy or noble, depending upon of course the total set of moral commitments she has.

Taylor has rightly made mention of two important aspects of the strong evaluator's moral personality: one, the deep sense of values she has, and second, the total plan of life she projects along with her deep moral commitments. The first aspect highlights the fact that the strong moral evaluator differs from the weak evaluator on the ground that the latter suffers from a lack of deep sense of values. The weak evaluator knows the utility of the things, but does not know the value of anything. She in fact lacks the value-sense altogether, or has only a very marginal one. This makes her the evaluator in a weak sense. The second aspect of the strong evaluator's personality touches on the total scheme of moral life she has, that is, the total set of moral values and commitments she entertains. This aspect brings out the underlying depth of her personality in a more articulate way. Taylor writes:

> Strong evaluation is not just a condition of articulacy about preferences, but also about the quality of life, the kind of beings we are or want to be. It is in this sense deeper.[14]

---

13. *The Self*, p. 114.
14. *Ibid.*, p. 115.

This is to reiterate that the quality of life depends upon how deep one's understanding of, and the commitment to, the values is. If the evaluator has no sense of higher values, then her total life-plan becomes shallow.

One cannot but agree with Taylor that it is the higher sense of values which holds the key to the quality of one's moral evaluation. The characteristic depth one manifests in one's evaluatory activities marks the strong evaluator as a strong moral person or agent. But it is to be further articulated in what the higher sense of values consists. Besides, it must be explained how a moral agent acquires this value-sense. The idea of commitment that we have introduced earlier helps us in identifying the higher sense of values. The higher values are so-called not because they have an origin outside life or have a divine sanction, though most of the religious values have a divine authority about them. For purely moral values what is required is that they be sanctioned by our reason and our total understanding of life. This brings in the idea of moral commitment or moral obligation which makes moral life a document of value-commitments. For example, respect for life is a value-commitment which all moral systems prescribe and therefore it is obligatory on our part to be loving towards all life. This moral attitude or commitment has a deep role to play in the ethics of non-violence. Thus, the higher values have something to do with the meaning and sanctity of life as such.

As to the question how the moral agents acquire the higher sense of values, it is to be noted that those who have a value-sense are after all human agents and that they have the potential value-sense as they live in the community of agents. This sense has to be cultivated and made more articulate so that the human agent qualifies to be a strong evaluator. The aim is to raise an agent to the level of strong moral personality which is found in all developed moral persons. Thus, the development of the moral personality depends on how the agent deepens her moral consciousness and how the higher value-sense becomes the moral habit with her. The value-sense is acquired in the sense that nobody is equipped with the moral sense from birth. Society inculcates the value-sense and awakens the rational faculty of valuation through training and moral education.

The idea of strong evaluation has thus the following presuppositions which need be articulated. They are as follows:

1. The moral agent presupposes the system of values which she is trained to imbibe and manifest in her value-judgements. The value-system is rationally and consciously adopted after a process of critical evaluation.
2. The values themselves have a unity and coherence which make them the values of a specific value-framework. There is an organic unity which binds them into a system. It is the intrinsic among them which deserve to be central, while the rest can belong to the periphery of the system.
3. Values are not man-made in the sense an artifact is man-made, but they are deeply ingrained in the human value-consciousness. Values are there just because without them we cannot have the value-consciousness. For example, the values of non-violence and respect for life are ingrained in the higher-order consciousness of man as it is the very bedrock of human existence.

Objectivity of values

The values that inform the value-consciousness of the moral agent must themselves be objective in the sense that if a value is not objectively there, it is difficult, nay, impossible that there be a value-consciousness at all. Values therefore have an existence as the objective value-entities. J.L. Mackie[15] of course argues that such a blanket granting of objective existence to values is the result of an error and therefore the objectivity argument in value theory is an error theory. Despite the sharpness of the error theory, it is obvious that values need a sanctuary in

---

15. J.L. Mackie, *Ethics: Inventing Right and Wrong*, (Penguin, Harmondsworth, 1977).

the moral realm for ethical judgements to be right or wrong, justified or unjustified. If rationality of the value-judgments is not a matter of critical thought and if anything can pass in the name of values, then Mackie's error theory could be taken for granted. But this is not the case in much of our moral evaluations. Moral evaluations require the supposition of moral values, and the moral critical thought grants that there be value-objectivity.

The division of values into the intrinsic (absolute) and insturmental (relative) is as old as moral thought. This division is made on the basis that certain values are values for their own sake, that is, they are objectively real on their own rather than because of their utility. This makes the intrinsic values the absolute values, e.g., respect for life, non-violence, etc. The instrumental values are so-called because of their utility and usefulness for something else, e.g., healthy, social stability, etc. It is the latter that are very often taken as the primary values but actually they subserve the higher interests of mankind. Therefore, it is the absolute values that need to be objectively situated for the sake of the possibility of moral evaluation. The absolute values alone can make the instrumental values worthy of our critical appreciation. In themselves the instrumental values have to be transcended by the absolute values.

Thomas Nagel[16] has expressed the apprehension that there is always a deeper conflict between the subjective and the objective perspective of values since on the one hand values are values for the individual agents and so are subjective in origin and yet on the other hand they have to be objective as they have to be agent-neutral. Thus there are two perspectives from which the values could be seen: from the perspective of the agent and from the perspective of the world at large which includes other human perspectives. Nagel's argument is that there is an uneasy truce between the two perspectives as they

---

16. Cf. Nagel, *op. cit.*, chapter VIII.

unhappily co-exit since they pull in opposite directions. The perspective of the agent is such that it cannot allow itself to be appropriated by the objective perspective of the world. The objective perspective itself cannot be denied because in that case there cannot be any value-discourse at all. Besides, unless objectivity is established, values cannot appear more than as subjective fancies. Thus, there is a seeming paradoxicality about our value-discourse as values are not completely subjective nor are they completely objective.

Nagel's argument seems flawed on the following grounds. First of all, he takes it for granted that the agents are solely responsible for the values they pursue and that the values are available only within the subjective perspective. Secondly, he believes that the objectivity of the values is constructed through a transcendence of the subjective perspective. Hence the objectivity of values follows as a result of the dissolution of the first-person perspective. But both the grounds are contestable. It is not the case that values have a subjective origin like knowledge, belief, experience, etc. Values have no origin in subjective consciousness, though the knowledge of values definitely has. Values as such are those that have a non-perspectival existence. That is why the objectivity of the values is built-into the nature of the values. Values therefore are either objective or nothing. Subjective values are not values at all. Values have essentially a trans-agential character.

In this context, it can be argued that values are transcendental in origin in the sense that they have to be always placed outside the contingent facts. Values are such that they transcend the facts in that they pertain to the meaning or the normativity of the facts. Norms and the facts cannot be placed on a par. If the values are assimilated into the facts, they cease to be values at all. Wittgenstein puts this characteristically in the following way:

> If there is any value that does have value, it must lie outside the whole sphere of what happens and is the case. For all that happens and is the case is accidental.[17]

---

17. Wittgenstein, *Tractatus Logico-Philosophicus*, tr. D.F. Pears and B.F. McGuinness, (Routledge and Kegan Paul, London, 1961), 6.41.

This is to say, values have to be kept away from the facts because the facts are accidental and do not share the essentiality and necessity of values. Thus, the values are transcendent to the facts.

To put it less metaphysically, values have a different origin from the facts. Values are ideals which do not have a factual existence at all, whereas the facts are in the world. Besides, the values are to be practised and made a matter of our value-consciousness. Thus, values have a logic of their own that matches with that of the ethical imperatives rather than that of the factual statements. No descriptive mechanism can capture the values, since the latter are prescriptive and ideal in character. We can therefore grant an ideal existence to the values rather than a factual and historical existence. Of course, it has been argued, amongst others by Putnam[18] that values are not sharply distinguishable from facts since the values themselves have a base in the factual history of the world. Besides, it is argued, values share with the facts the trait of being critically evaluated and revised in the light of new experience. Thus, the facts and values both have elements of being man-made and progressively improved upon. It must, however, be admitted that in spite of Putnam's bridging the gulf between values and facts, the distinction still remains and the elements of normativity have to be granted even in the otherwise contingent facts of history.

The value-commitments which define our value-consciousness have to be admitted precisely for the reason that there are objectively real values. In the absence of the objective values, it is difficult to establish that the moral agents have strong commitment to values. The subjective values cannot create any sense of obligation on the part of the agent. Therefore, it must be admitted that the objective values are the only values available for the moral agent.

---

18. See Hilary Putnam, *Reason, Truth and History*, (Cambridge University Press, Cambridge, 1981), chapter 6.

The valuational system and the second-order desires

It must be granted to Nagel that the agent's value-commitments are part of the valuational system the agents imbibe rather than of the value-system as such. The agent is autonomous in evolving her valuational system, that is, she can have a very personal valuational system and can define her value-commitments. But the values themselves must be agent-neutral. It is because the valuational system can be constructed and improved upon, whereas the values have to be relatively stable and fixed.

The valuational system is internal to the agent's value-consciousness and is part of the conceptual framework which the agent operates. The valuational system includes the standards, norms and the rules which the agent follows but under the agent's ciritical evalution. Therefore, the agent has the freedom to decide which valuational system to choose. She is free to decide whether she has to have only one valuational system or many. If she chooses many, she is likely to be more liberal and flexible. But if she has only one such system, she is likely to be dogmatic. But this choice is limited only to the valuational system, but not to the values themselves. Values are absolute, but not the valuational system. The agent has no freedom to make values, though she has the freedom to choose to adopt any value. This proves that the agential perspective is still a matter of importance.

The valuational system is the system of the agent's desires, intentions, preferences, etc., which go to constitute his moral psyche. The valuational preferences are laid down in the moral dispositions of the agent so that she makes her value-judgements according to her value-preferences. The latter are basically the psychological propensities which the agent carries with her. Though they are subjective, yet they have a public manifestation in the activities of the agent. The agent accumulates the value-preferences over a long period of time and forms what we have called the valuational system. This, therefore, becomes internal to the individual agent's moral belief-desire system.

In this connection, it is natural to recognise the possibility of the second-order desires and other higher-order thoughts as part of the valuational system. Taylor, following Frankfurt,[19] admits that there are second-order desires which the agent evolves as a part of her moral personality. It is argued that the first-order desires have to be guided and evaluated by the second-order desires in that the latter are born out of the reflective consciousness of the agent. For example, the desire for a forbidden food is the first-order desire and the desire to curb this desire and to evaluate it in terms of its consequences is a second-order desire. It is the latter that is morally significant because at this level the agent is aware of the value of a certain desire. Taylor writes:

> I agree with Frankfurt that this capacity to evaluate desires is bound up with our power of self-evaluation, which in turn is an essential feature of the mode of agency we recognise as human.[20]

That is to say that the second-order desires fall within the sphere of our reflective awareness in the sense that in this sphere alone the first-order desires are evaluated. The reflective awareness itself is a value-awareness in the sense that because of this awareness there is the sense of the higher and lower, noble and ignoble among the desires. The moral agent chooses the higher and the nobler among the desires and thus builds up her second-order desires.

However, it must be acknowledged that the second-order desires are not desire proper, since the agent does not any more indulge in these desires. The reflective moral sense transcends the indulgent desires and thus manifests the capacity not to have those desires that limit the agent to a lower level of existence. This happens in all cases of transmutation and

---

19. H. Frankfurt, "Freedom of the Will and the Concept of a Person", *Journal of Philosophy*, LXVII, No. 1, 1971, pp. 5-20.

20. Taylor, *op. cit.*, p. 104.

transformation of the ordinary desires. A case in point is the renunciation of the worldly life on the part of great saints and moral geniuses. Their first-order desire for worldly life is denied for the sake of a higher life the sense of which is a part of their second-order desire. The *Bhagavad Gita* conception of the renunciation of the desire for the fruits of an action is an instance of a second-order desire for not indulging in the fruits of the action.

The Frankfurt-Taylor conception of a second-order desire is inadequate to bring in the sense of the moral commitments and the notion of the strong evaluator. It is because this conception of a second-order desire is not logically connected with the moral valuational consciousness. The latter is born out of the reflective consciousness no doubt but it is not itself sufficient. The moral commitments are deeply-laid moral inclinations of the agent and so it is not the case that the value-consciousness is so easily reflected in our so-called second-order desires. Second-order desires may simply be the mechanical activities of classifying the desires and placing them under the category of the lower and the higher. But the agent may fail to choose the higher desires and thus may show utter disregard for the higher values of life. Taylor has, however, argued that the agent who fails to commit herself to the higher values may be called the weak evaluator and so dismissed as a moral agent. But the fact remains that the strong evaluator may similarly have only mechanical interest in the higher values and may not herself practise them. In this situation the best suggestion could be that the total moral personality of the moral agent has to be taken into account and not her second-order desires alone. Taylor is right in emphasising that the quality of life of the agent has to be the touchstone of the moral agent's strong evaluatory character.

The most appropriate suggestion in this regard could be that we locate the value-commitments in the higher region of our valuational consciousness such that we find a greater meaning in the notion of self-transcendence. Self-transcendence could provide the necessary ground not only for second-order desires but also for higher order moral motivations. That could provide a greater avenue to full-fledged value-consciousness.

Self-transcendence

The capacity for self-transcendence is typical of the human agents and it is *sine qua non* for the moral agents. In self-transcendence lies the rise of the value-consciousness. It is this that takes us beyond the natural desire and motives. We get the maximal sense of self-improvement in this urge for self-transcendence.

Our urge for self-transcendence arises when we commit ourselves to the forward-looking actions. Most of our actions are forward-looking because we commit ourselves to their execution in some future time. This commitment to the future plans, goals and actions makes us typical human agents. In a sense we live in the future as much as we live in the present. The present is only a link to the future in terms of our projects and actions. Moya puts it as follows:

> Meaningful actions imply, then, the existence of subjects able to commit themselves to do things in the future. I shall contend that this notion of commitment is essential to our notion of agency. . . . It constitutes an essential part of our idea of ourselves as agents, as beings who are able to change the world and not mere victims of its evolution.[21]

Thus, the agent transcends her present for the sake of the future and becomes a true agent in the sense that future responsibilities have to be included in her agency. This is more true of the moral agents who commit themselves deliberately to future goals and consequences.

The second important aspect of self-transcendence lies in the overcoming of our lower desires and motives for the sake of a higher life. This is reflected in the life of every civilised human being. The higher we ascend the more civilised we are.

---

21. Moya, *op. cit.*, p. 46.

Thus, the moral perfection is the ideal goal of all civilised existence. The Upanishadic sense of the dictinction between the *shreyas* and the *preyas* is typical of the moral sense of the distinction between the higher and the lower values and the commitments. The higher ideals have the promise of the perfectibility of our moral self. That is why psychology recognises the fact that man's value-aspiration is built into her moral agency.

The higher moral consciousness is only a step away from what Sri Aurobindo[22] calls the universal cosmic consciousness which all morally evolved human beings aspire for. It is this aspiration that charaterises the consciousness of an integrated, self-conscious human individual who affiliates herself to the cosmic self. Thus, self-consciousness and self-transcendence become full-fledged in the realisation of the cosmic meaning of our existence. Sri Aurobindo writes:

> Man is shut up at present in his surface individual consciousness and knows the world only through his outward mind and senses and by interpreting their contacts with the world. By *yoga* there can open up in him a consciousness which becomes one with that of the world; he becomes directly aware of a universal Being, universal States, universal Force and Power, universal Mind, Life, Matter and lives in conscious relation with these things. He is then said to have cosmic consciousness.[23]

This picture of the universal consciousness may look highly metaphysical but it is not very different from what we have so far called the higher value-consciousness. It is only words away from the inner world of self-transcendence.

Concluding remarks

We arrive at the following conclusions so far as our notion of moral agency is concerned. They are:

---

22. See Sri Aurobindo, *Life Divine*, 2 Vols., (Sri Aurobindo Ashram, Pondicherry, 1973).

23. Sri Aurobindo, *A Practical Guide to Integral Yoga*, (Sri Aurobindo Ashram, Pondicherry, 1955: Reprinted, 1995), pp. 24-5.

1. The moral self or agent has the aspiration to go to the higher levels of value-consciousness depending upon her value-commitments.

2. The higher value-consciousness emerges out of the evaluatory consciousness found in the moral agents.

3. The moral agent is the repository of the value-consciousness and the value-commitments. It is these that make her a moral agent. The cosmic self is only a metaphysical extension of the value-aspiring and self-transcending self.

To sum up: to be a moral agent is to be fully committed to the higher-order value-consciousness. Thus, valuational consciousness and self-transcendence go together.

3

Fact/Value Holism and the Ethics of Human Freedom

Amitabha Das Gupta

A false move

THE concept of freedom and its elucidation has been always a source of perplexity. The perplexity arises due to the dual nature of the concept. On the one hand, this concept has an abstract nature. It is an irreducibly normative concept forming the very core of the mental subjectivity of man. But, at the same time, it is a situational concept pointing out its existential nature and thus it is felt that freedom is the description of man in the world. This is the dual nature of the concept which leads to a tension. It is a tension between the two standpoints of freedom. But how far is this tension real? Apparently, of course, there is nothing to doubt since the two different standpoints of freedom follow from its dual nature. But one may question the very characterisation of freedom defined in terms of its dual nature. It is quite possible that freedom does not have any dual nature. Duality of freedom is a misconception. It arises as a result of our reconstruction of the concept. True, no one can deny the situational nature of the concept. But freedom, as pointed out, is irreducibly a normative concept forming the core of agency, cannot be defined in any situational/external terms. Freedom is something internal belonging to the mental subjectivity of man. Such a picture is indeed a reconstruction of freedom divorced from the idea of freedom we live by. As a consequence of this, we find freedom is either traditionally taken as a metaphysical concept implying that it is a state of mind, or, in contemporary terms, freedom is understood within the perspective of the moral psychology of individuals implying that freedom consists in holding certain attitudes or it is a capacity to evaluate our desires. This is an internalist perspective of freedom against which determinism comes as a natural opposition — an irreconcilable antithesis to freedom. The notion of freedom has been thus always construed in terms of its opposites. As a result, in the discussion on freedom we invariably encounter with such pair of opposites like: freedom and determinism, free will and causality, subjective and objective, internal and external, etc.

At this point, there is a methodological question involved here. It is a question concerning the basis — the source from which these pair of opposites are derived. There must be a framework — a methodological design within which these pairs assume their significance and, more importantly, their justification. It is the fact/value dichotomy that provides defence to these pairs of opposites. It is the basis from which they are derived. The point that I am making is that the internalist perspective on freedom which defines freedom necessarily in terms of its opposites is supported by an underlying methodology — the methodology of fact/value dichotomy.

The main argument of this paper is to question the internalist perspective of freedom and to show that defining freedom in terms of its opposites is a speculative exercise with having little or no connection with freedom we experience in the world. The various pairs of opposites are more like conceptual distinctions. Whereas in actual existential terms there are no such opposites. The very idea of existential freedom includes all of them. Determinism is not an antithesis to freedom because the two are intertwined. The alternative conception of freedom that I am going to defend conceives freedom as embodied, meaning thereby, that there is freedom only in a situation — in a social space. Since freedom is always embodied there is nothing called freedom *per se* and, hence, we find that freedom is necessarily intermixed with conflicting element such as, determinism. Freedom is thus not a well defined notion.

However, the proposed alternative conception of freedom will not be defendable unless we change the underlying methodology that involves a fact/value dichotomy. The internalist perspective of freedom assumes this fact/value dichotomy. Without the latter the former cannot stand. Similarly, for its support, the alternative conception of freedom demands an alternative methodology. Instead of fact/value dichotomy the new methodology involves fact/value holism.

In view of the stated objectives the paper will have three sections. The first section of the paper will briefly point out what is wrong with the internalist perspective of freedom. In this respect, it will be particularly interested to show that the fact/value dichotomy which is presupposed in the internalist perspective is responsible for certain untenable views. The second section will spell out how is fact/value holism possible. The third section, on the basis of fact/value holism, will offer a new conception of freedom.

I

What is wrong with the internalist perspective of freedom?

In contemporary terms, the account offered by the internalist perspective of freedom is mostly based within the perspective of moral psychology of individuals. In this respect, there have been two celebrated accounts, offered by Peter Strawson and the other offered by Charles Taylor. The two are different accounts in the sense that each is addressing to a different issue. Thus, Strawson is interested in defining the concept of a person and what constitutes the freedom of a person. Whereas, Taylor is interested in defining what constitutes the moral agency of an individual. But both the accounts though different are conceived within the same internalist perspective supported by the underlying methodology of fact/value dichotomy. The account offered by Strawson is more general arguing that freedom is situated in the internal life of an individual. Whereas the account offered by Taylor is much more specific concentrating on the particular aspect of human freedom, namely, the notion of moral agent. I shall now give a brief account of both these views in order to show what is wrong with them.

Freedom and its opposites: Strawson's internalist account

'What is person?' is the central question that Strawson[1] asked while giving his account on freedom. If freedom is not metaphysically grounded, then the main problem of freedom, for Strawson, is: Where do we situate freedom?, and: How do we do it? This is how one comes to the notion of a person and the constitution of it.

Person is not an objective fact in the way in which things or material bodies of the world are. The distinctiveness of a person, on the other hand, lies in having a set of attitudes which Strawson calls 'reactive' or 'participant' attitudes. An individual is called a person because of these attitudes and thus it is true that without them there cannot be any idea of a person. Strawson mentioned a few instances of such attitudes and responses. They are gratitude, love, resentment, hurt feelings, forgiveness, moral indignation, etc. These are obviously reciprocal attitudes figured in interpersonal communication. The attitude which I express towards others is the same attitude which they reciprocate towards me. This is how we form the intersubjective attitudinal space which is responsible for the intersubjective relations among people in the society.

In Strawson's argument, human freedom is essentially grounded in these attitudes. The idea that an individual is a free moral agent can be found only in relation to these attitudes since, as Strawson observes, these are the attitutes which

1. P.F. Strawson, *Freedom and Resentment and other Essays*, (Methuen, London, 1974).

form the part of our moral life. Moral life does not constitute a separate domain nor does freedom has a separate existence. These interpersonal attitudes are fundamental to what a person is and they form the basic structure of our moral life including the idea of a free agent. Instead of searching for freedom *per se*, we should look into these attitudes because they are the expressions of freedom and agency.

The significance of these reactive attitudes can be better seen in opposition to what Strawson calls objective attitudes. From the point of view of objective attitudes a person is essentially seen as an object "to be managed or handled or cured or trained".[2] This is a scientific/external approach reducing a person to an object. The subject becomes the object of manipulation. This results in the total destruction of the internal life of a person and thus he will be incapable of entering into any interpersonal relationship.

To probe further into Strawson's argument, the objective attitude is closely linked with universal determinism — the belief that all actions are causally determined. To hold this will be to deny the idea of freedom and responsibility which are the inalienable properties of human persons. A person can be neither blamed nor praised for his action since all his actions are predetermined. Similarly, in such a framework we cannot expect an agent to respond appropriately to our reactions. This is not possible because the agent will no longer be a free agent. This is certainly a reductionism which Strawson questioned and asked at this point whether such a whole scale reductionism is possible or not. Strawson has ruled out such a possibility because we cannot imagine a situation in which our ordinary interpersonal attitudes will cease to exist. We cannot imagine because our commitment to these attitudes "form the part of our general framework of human life".[3] To deny these attitudes will be thus to deny human life.

---

2. *Freedom and Resentment and other Essays*, p. 68.
3. *Ibid.*, p. 70.

The reactive and the objective attitudes are the two ways of looking at ourselves. They may be accordingly called the internal and external perspectives of human agency. Strawson does not leave these two viewpoints as they are. He takes a definite side and, accordingly, defends it. In his argument, the acceptance of reactive attitudes is necessary. It is necessary because it forms the precondition of moral reality as well as of our moral life. Morality will be impossible without accepting the fact that man is a free agent. The important epistemological feature of this standpoint is that it derives its justification from itself. The consequence of it is that the internal perspective which consists of reactive attitudes is neutral to any criticism made from objective standpoint. It will be logically misplaced if we bring the latter standpoint for the assessment of the former. But at the same time we should also remember that Strawson is not ruling out the possibility of these attitudes to be assessed. But the assessment must be made "inside the general structure or web of human attitude".[4] The justification or criticism to be offered must be internal because "an external rational justification" of these attitudes is not permissible.

These are Strawson's arguments which constitute his answer to the question: What is it like to be a person? He adopted a strategy which carefully demarcates the internal and the external aspects of human subjects. Freedom is internal to man and its presence is felt due to those reactive attitudes. This is an attempt which elucidates a general conception of freedom that presupposes the acceptance of fact/value distinction at its very foundation. This is evident from Strawson's distinction between two types of attitudes resulting into the distinction between freedom and determinism. His criticism of Schlick's view on human freedom in terms of causal explanation is a further elaboration of the stand that freedom is something intrinsic to person and thus it cannot be reduced to anything external expressing the objective standpoint. Freedom is thus necessarily conceived in terms of its opposites, which is

4. *Freedom and Resentment and other Essays*, p. 71.

supported by the underlying methodology of fact/value dichotomy.

In my introductory remarks, I have already said that the attempt to define freedom in terms of its opposites is a false move. Freedom is not opposed to determinism. It is, on the other hand, coextensive with it. The reason for saying this is that freedom cannot be kept separately from the situation outside. By freedom, on the other hand, we normally understand freedom in a situation. To accept this will be to accept both freedom and its opposites. The reason is to see freedom in a situation implies that there will be nothing called pure freedom. Freedom will be necessarily intermixed along with all the diversities of a situation. That there can't be any pure freedom with having a place of its own is the objection that we are holding against Strawson. I shall now give three arguments to show the untenability of the internalist conception of freedom that Strawson advocates.

Withering away the opposites

First: Strawson while defending his internalist idea of freedom assumes that as if freedom has an absolute nature. Freedom is not constrained by external factors. Any assessment of freedom must be done internally. But can we have such absolute, in the sense of pure notion of freedom undisturbed by the external/ objective standpoint? Possibly not. As Ernest Nagel[5] pointed out, Strawson's conception of freedom involves an anomalous situation. According to Nagel, to adopt the objective standpoint means treating ourselves as part of the natural world. It will be a world where we may not be praised or blamed for our actions because they will be treated as natural events. True that these two standpoints — external and internal, are different. But, as Nagal observes, they are not discontinuous because both belong to the same framework — "the framework of human life". That is the reason why objective viewpoint is never alien to our life

5. E. Nagel, *The View From Nowhere*, (Oxford University Press, 1986).

and this is reflected in our outlook – our craving for being objective. This is the situation where we no longer confine ourselves only to the internal perspective but place ourselves to the wider world and critically examine our own reactive attitudes from that point of view. This is how we get more and more objective understanding about our own selves. This is also the requirement of freedom since without critical self-understanding we cannot act in the best possible way. But what do we get at the end of this objective path? In Nagel's observation, we are thrown into an anomalous situation. On the one hand, we find that in order to achieve self-understanding for the sake of freedom we need to be objective and, on the other hand, we find that this pursuit for self-understanding ultimately becomes the death knell to freedom. This happens because the whole idea of individual self ceases to exist. It merges with the outside world. This, indeed, is an irreconcilable situation expressing what Nagel says "skepticism and helplessness".[6]

I am not interested in the dispute between Strawson and Nagel nor am I in complete agreement with Nagel. In the context of this paper the significance lies over the point that Nagel is raising. The kind of anomaly that we find in Strawson's conception of freedom points out that freedom cannot be placed separately divorced from any external contact. Similarly, the notion of pure freedom is a mere theoretical abstraction with having little or no contact with reality. If there is no place for absolute freedom then on the same ground there cannot be any distinction between the internal and the external standpoint. In view of this, freedom cannot be conceived in terms of its opposites since the theory supporting these opposites is itself under attack.

However, all these findings do not suggest that we should subscribe to Nagel's pessimism. Nagel described the situation as hopeless because he could not resolve the anomaly. In our

---

6. E. Nagel, *The View From Nowhere*, p. 120.

assessment anomaly arises due to particular conception of freedom that we hold. We have inherited from our metaphysical past that freedom has a separate place in the internal life of man. It is further thought that the only alternative to this is determinism. Hence, there is either freedom or determinism. This sharp dichotomy that is posed here is indeed the result of fact/value dichotomy. If, on the other hand, we have a different conception of value where values will not be antagonistic to fact we will have a different conception of freedom — a freedom that will be free from any anomaly and at the same time it will not be identified with determinism.

Second: The second argument against Strawson's internalist conception of freedom says that freedom has certain limitations or restrictions. They are not obstacles to freedom. They will be viewed as obstacles only if we take freedom in the absolute sense of the term. On the other hand, the presence of these restrictions will be necessarily felt whenever there is a situation involving freedom. As said earlier, there is freedom only in a situation and thus the first restriction of freedom is that it is restricted or limited to a situation. Along with this, freedom is limited to our capacities. There are things which we can do and, similarly, there are things which we cannot do. Thirdly. freedom is limited to knowledge. If we take freedom in relation to a situation then knowledge of the situation is important for the exercise of freedom. My ability to exercise freedom in a given situation is thus limited to my knowledge of the situation.

Apart from the fact that freedom is limited to these three, there is another siginificant feature of freedom that deserves to be mentioned in this connection. Normally, we take freedom to be opposed to anything mechanical. Freedom in this sense is opposed to habits and the acquisition of skills which form the mechanical part of our human behaviour. But this idea is wrong. It has come from the same source that freedom must be conceived in terms of its opposites. The behavioural repertoire consisting of acquired responses and patterns is the one through which we bacame involved with this world. We become conscious of the environment on the basis of the accumulated skills and habits. By being conscious of it we also become conscious of the fact that our existence is grounded on the vast depository of mechanical experience and habits. Though it is a highly impersonal experience is, nevertheless, there as the essential part of being-in-the-world. We realise that this is a necessary fact of human existence and through this we acquire a mental space which makes us free from our environment. Mechanical experience which is described in the phenomenological literature as sedimentation[7] is not opposite to freedom. It is, on the other hand, providing the ground of freedom. Freedom is the urge to transcend — to transcend the existing structure and to create a new one. Freedom is modelled on our understanding of the experience of sedimentation. It is thus an emerging phenomenon. It emerges from the mechanical structures of human existence.

Third: The third argument says that freedom cannot be confused with free will. That freedom implies free will is the well accepted thesis of the internalist. This is the view where we see the clear separation between freedom and its opposites. The dichotomy between free will and determinism is the outcome of this separation. True, we find that there is a dichotomy; but dichotomy arises because we see freedom in isolation from any social situation. Whereas, the same dichotomy will be found to be unreal once we see freedom in a situation, i.e., to see freedom as embodied. The dichotomy between free will and determinism is unreal because man can be neither said to be completely determined nor can he be said to have absolute free will. The justification of such a claim can be found if we look at human action. Actions are neither caused nor uncaused. We do something because there is some reason for it or there may be a purpose to achieve. Actions may be thus described as intentional. The advocates of determinism wrongly think

---

7. M. Merleau-Ponty, *The Primacy of Perception and other Essays*, (North Western University Press, Evanston, 1964), p. 86.

that the only alternative to determinism is chaos. Their main argument is: the order and intelligibility that the world exhibits shows that everything in this world must be determined or predetermined. This is not so, because the intelligibility of the world is not result of any form of determinism. The world is structured by us and we do it according to our own dispositions. It is we who create social rules and patterns and canons of intelligibility while acting with each other. In a similar way we can argue from the perspective of human action that freedom does not imply an unconstrained act of the will. We judge an action by looking at its quality. It is the quality of action and not will that is what matters in our evaluation. Freedom and determinism do not form a pair of opposites. There is no opposition between the two. The two terms are thus co-extensive.

What is it like to be a moral agent?

Strawson in his attempt to situate the notion of freedom asked the question: What is it like to be a human person? In a similar vein, Charles Tylor[8] asked the question: What is it like to be a free moral agent? His attempt may be said to be an exploration seeking to discover the constitution of moral self. As a result, the notion of responsibility is placed at the centre of his notion of freedom. A free agent is one who is a morally responsible person.

Taylor defines freedom as the capacity to evaluate our own desires. This is a capacity which is distinctive of man because animals do not have this capacity. Taylor by following the distinction made by Frankfurt, describes this capacity for reflective self-evaluation as second order desire. The very act of evaluation involves a desire — the desire to evaluate my having first order desires. These are actual desires which are subjected to evaluation by the agent *qua* moral agent. Since

---

8. C. Taylor, "What is Human Agency?" in his *Human Agency and Language, Philosophical Papers I*, (Cambridge University Press, 1985).

freedom implies evaluation of desires and since evaluation involves moral responsibility, freedom thus consists in being a responsible moral agent. Freedom becomes coextensive with responsibility. Taylor makes a further distinction while going into the details of the process involved in evaluation. There may be evaluation in two senses – the weak and the strong sense. The weak evaluation is a matter of weighing the different desires so that by doing it I can decide which desire can give me the maximum result. In this process other desires are pushed to the background because they are found to be incompatible or conflicting with the present one. Now what really decides the matter is the outcome, and, it is in the light of the outcome that other altenatives are rejected. Alternatives are thus imcompatible not on any intrinsic ground but on the ground of its outcome. This may be described as outcome evaluation where evaluation is a matter of calculation. The strong evaluation, on the other hand, is concerned with the qualitative worth of desires. This means to say that desires are judged not in terms of their outcome but in terms of their intrinsic worth. I do not, for example, allow myself from acting on a given motive, say envy, because I consider this as unworthy or cowardice. Note that doing this action will be otherwise beneficial to me. But I refrain to do this on a moral ground not on the ground of outcome. My evaluation is thus said to be concerned with the quality of motivation. This qualitative dimension is absent in weak evaluation. Nor this qualitative dimension be reduced to calculation which the utilitarians try to do. In the context of strong evaluation my decisions for one alternative among the several will defy any quantification. The reason is that I am essentially concerned with the qualitative worth of the desires. Taylor argues that human agency is fundamentally characterised by strong evaluative consideration of worth. In our life we do consider some desires or ways of life as higher or worthier than others. We articulate our preference by making evaluative judgements. These judgements together with desire, feeling and action make a kind of depth that is distinctive of human life as we understand it.

An equally important feature of strong evaluation is that it involves the notion of responsibility. The way persons are held responsible animals are not. That we think of a person as responsible is an essential feature of a moral agent. As Taylor argues, this feature too is connected with our capacity to evaluate desires. An agent is held responsible for what he does – "for the degree to which he acts in line with his evaluation". But he is also responsible for his evaluation. Taylor argues that this idea follows from the conceptual meaning of the word 'evaluation'. Grammatically, the word 'evaluation' implies the verb 'to evaluate' which suggests performing an action. Our evaluations are thus inseparably related to our activity of evaluation where the former follows from the latter. "In this sense", as Taylor observes, "we are responsible."[9]

The problem now is how to understand this particular mode of responsibility involved in the evaluation of desires. The one influential approach which seeks to understand this is the theory of radical choice by Sartre. In Taylor's argument radical choice cannot account for strong evaluation. The reason is that a radical choice cannot justify the desirability of one alternative over the other. A choice which is unrelated to its alternatives will not be intelligible as a choice. A radical choice since it lacks justification cannot be a case of strong evaluation. Whereas, the proponents of radical choice theory want to maintain both strong evaluation and radical choice together, without offering proper justification. In Taylor's assessment, this brings incoherence to the position expressed by radical choice theory. Strong evaluation does not imply radical choice.

The strong evaluation involves responsibility. The responsibility lies on our choosing – choosing the most desired one from the set of alternatives. I try to assess the qualitative worth of the various alternatives. Deciding the worth and giving justification of it is crucial to evaluation. This is how I become responsible for what I choose while making evaluation in the

9. *Human Agency and Language*, p. 28.

strong sense. There is a significant point to be noted here. As Taylor points out, the justification of the worth of an alternative is usually expressed through the language of contrast. Thus, the superiority of one alternative over another may be described by using such pairs of opposites like: "higher and lower, noble and base, courageous and cowardly, integrated and fragmented and so on".[10]

We could now see how, according to Taylor, freedom essentially means the capacity to evaluate desires on the ground of moral worth. This way the process of evaluation involves the notion of responsibility. Taylor, thus understands by freedom as responsibility and concludes that a man who is free is a moral agent.

Taylor does not explicitly talk about the internal or the external perspective of freedom. He was not interested to situate freedom in the way in which Strawson was. But from his account of freedom it is evident that he is committing himself to the internalist notion of freedom. The whole idea of strong evaluation suggests that freedom is internal to man which is undisturbed by the situation outside. Accordingly, the act of evaluation and the responsibility involved in it are the part of the internal resources of man. They are pure and sharply demarcated notions independent of any factual consideration. The same fact/value dichotomy is presupposed at the back of this conception of freedom. But is there anything called pure evaluation? I shall argue that pure evaluation is an outcome of the internalist fallacy of freedom.

The myth of pure evaluation

There are two ways in which the act of evaluation and responsibility are connected. First, an agent is responsible for his action; we ask: How far his action is in line with his evaluation? Second, the evaluation that we make is the result of our activity of evaluation. Hence, in this sense, as Taylor

10. *Human Agency and Language*, p. 24.

claims, we are responsible. I shall now argue that these two are not tenable in view of the counter possibility. On the basis of this I shall show that neither there is any pure responsibility nor there is any pure evaluation.

Coming to the relationship between evaluation and responsibility, it is often found that there is no parity among the two. A difference is thus found between what we decide to do and the consequence of what we do. The reason is that we do not have complete control over the situation. As a result the meaning that I ascribe to my action may not be the same meaning that others ascribe to it. It is due to this discrepancy we find that there is no single interpretation of an action. All our actions are over determined in the sense that they admit of more than one interpretations. Thus, an agent may not necessarily have a clear-cut idea about his own action. These situations point out that due to these uncertainties the notion of responsibility may not have a clear-cut meaning. True, we have some freedom regarding what we do. But, at the same time, we must recognise the influence of other people on us. We are in constant interaction with other people and what we do is largely influenced by this interaction. Our actions are never performed in isolation from the actions of others. They are connected by a network of interrelated actions. For example, my present action may be motivated by a prior action of someone. Actions are thus to a great extent interpersonal in nature. In view of this, it is difficult to maintan that there is anything called pure responsibility.

But, can there by anything called pure evaluation? Taylor's idea of evaluation assumes that evaluation as an act has a separate place and it is, thereby, unaffected by any empirical description. This is an indication of Taylor's acceptance of pure evaluation which maintains that evaluation and description are logically distinct. The acceptance of this entails that evaluation is totally devoid of descriptive content. But is this really so? If we look into the way in which evaluative terms are learnt we will find that they are essentially mixed up with certain empirical situations. The two vocabularies are intermixed. Even an innocuous example like saying: "Taylor is good and Clinton is sad" we are depending on specific empirical situations. To say this implies that we are saying something about them – something that is empirically different between the two. In fact, if need arises the entire statement can be substantiated by such details like: Clinton is a racist whereas Taylor is not. We can move on to abstract concepts, such as, noble, courageous, cowardly, etc., and we will find that the same principle holds. Taylor holds that an agent has a vocabulary of worth. He justifies the higher desirability of, say *A* and *B* by using this vocabulary. But are they purely valuational concepts? They are not. The reason is that values and facts are inseparably related. That is why the process of evaluation cannot be totally independent of empirical situation. We learn moral concepts in relation to empirical situation. They do not enjoy absolute autonomy. Just like there is no pure responsibility, in a similar way there is also no pure evaluation.

In my criticism of the internalist perspective of freedom I have rejected fact/value dichotomy thesis and in turn defended what I have called fact/value holism. This is an alternative methodology defending an alternative conception of freedom. But, so far, I did not spell out the composition of this holistic methodology nor the logical basis of it. This I shall do it in the next section.

II

The structural composition of fact/value holism

I have already remarked that fact/value dichotomy is an artificially created dichotomy without having a firm basis in our experience. I have, therefore, argued for fact/value holism implying the inseparability of the two. These two together create a holistic framework. What is the nature of this holism?, and, what is its structural composition? – are the questions to be now addressed. In the following discussion I shall briefly elaborate these points.

First: Description-based evaluation — It has been already pointed out that description and evaluation are not logically distinct activities. Evaluation can as well be description.[11] For example, the sentence[12] 'The room is comfortable' is an expression of my attitude — the attitude of my approval of the room. This is an evaluative statement because corresponding to it there is no empirical phenomena which can be identified as the part of the quality of being comfortable. True, there is no such single phenomenon existing but certainly there is a range of phenomena taken together can serve the purpose. To explain, when I say the room is comfortable, I mean, for example, the room is well lighted, airy and so on. This is what I understand by the meaning of the term 'comfortable'. This range of phenomena exhibit the quality of something (i.e., the room) being comfortable. The statement is thus both evaluative and descriptive. By saying that the room is comfortable, I am saying something about the room and at the same time by saying this I am expressing my attitude towards the room. This is a case of description-based evaluation.

Second: Evaluation-based description — An evaluatively neutral description of human action is not a logically viable proposition. It may be argued at two levels.[13] At the first level the argument may be given to show the untenability of pure description of human action. Description of human action is always context dependent. Description is always offered from a point of view. It is the particular point of view that influences me to look out for relevant facts. Further, an action is understandable or intelligible to us only by taking into account of the context of the action. Raising my hand may be meant either waving good-

---

11. A.R. Louch, *Explanation and Human Action*, (Blackwell, Oxford, 1966), chapter 3.

12. L. Spurling, *Phenomenology and the Social World*, (Routledge & Kegan Paul, London, 1977), p. 112.

13. J. Koversi, *Moral Notions*, (Routledge & Kegan Paul, London, 1987).

bye to someone or trying to attract the attention of someone. Actions are thus interpreted according to the context. Pure action will mean uninterpreted physical movement which cannot be recognised as action. There is no pure action. Facts in the social world are always contextual and the description of it are, therefore, always contextual.

The thesis that descriptions are contextual because facts are contextual gives rise to the idea of evaluation. When I describe an event by providing a context I am also at the same time assessing the event. The reason is proving the context implies that I am saying how the event is to be viewed. I can describe an event of someone committing a murder.[14] The description provides the entire context of how the murder took place and the intentional nature of the action. This description may look like a bare description because it is not a moral judgement. But this is not true because this description is also an assessment of the situation. The meaning of the word 'murder' is that it is morally wrong. The description of a murder cannot be value neutral. To describe it is also to assess it. The assessment follows from the language that is used. This is true of a large number of descriptive concepts whose use cannot be value neutral. The reason is that the idea of evaluation is rooted in the conceptual vocabulary expressed by our language. Language reveals that facts and values cannot be separated because description and evaluation cannot be separated.

Third: The social world is the moral world — The social world and the moral world are not isolated. They are intertwined. Language is the evidence to this intertwined nature of the two. Of course, one can question this and may hold that at a conceptual level there is a distinction between the meanings of evaluative and descriptive words. But such a distinction is untenable from the point of view of language use. After all, meaning to a large extent, is decided by the way the words are used. This is what we have seen from our earlier discussion.

14. L. Spurling, *Phenomenology and the Social World*, p. 114.

But the argument from language is only supplying the evidence to the view that social world is a moral world. It is not the ground showing how and why the social world can as well be regarded as the moral world. To provide such a ground is necessary because it will constitute the proper justification of the moral nature of the social world. Such a justification will provide a strong foundation of fact/value holism. The justification that I shall offer is the one which has been already offered in phenomenology. It is a phenomenological justification existing prior to the linguistic argument.

The justification that I am offering rests on Merleau-Ponty's idea of the primacy of perception.[15] Perception or perceptual experience is the original source of all our values, rationality, description and so on. Perception reveals me that there is a common world where there are people other than me existing. If perception is so primary to our existence and life then its primacy must be established.

Regarding the primacy of perception, the argument offered from phenomenology is that when I look at an object, I don't see it merely as physical. On the other hand, I see the object with having meaning or significance. I apprehend them as intentional. The idea that is involved here is that of a perceptual field created by the act of perception. It is a field where there is no distinction between perceptual objects (facts) and the way I perceive them (value). Perceptual objects are there by virtue of my perceiving them and I perceive them according to my own ideas, orientation and moorings. Objects in this sense are evaluated. In perceptual field since there is no conflict between objects and the way I see it there is no distinction between fact and value or between is and ought. Here emerges an interesting fact/value synthesis. Perceptual field is originally pre-objective. Objects are brought into this field by the act of perception. Perception thus reduces the gap between the subjective and the objective. This is how Hume's antinomy is

---

15. M. Merleau-Ponty, *The Primacy of Perception and other Essays.*

by-passed.[16] Thus the idea of a perceptual field could provide the ground — a foundation to the belief that social world is a moral world where evaluative discourse and descriptive discourse are not logically distinct. I tried to show in this discussion the structural composition of fact/value holism on the basis of two types of arguments — phenomenological and linguistic.

III

Freedom: To be true to myself

I have all through argued that freedom cannot be conceived as having a separate place which is internal to man. To argue this is to argue against the internalist perspective of freedom. As against the internalist conception of freedom, I have, on the other hand, tried to defend a conception of freedom according to which freedom is necessarily embodied implying that there is freedom only in a situation. This idea of freedom has been supported by the underlying methodology involving fact/value holism. But I have not, so far, elaborated the nature of this notion of freedom. This will be offering a description of what is meant by embodied freedom in constructive terms. In my attempt, freedom will be thus understood as authenticity.

As said earlier, to see freedom as embodied is to see freedom in a situation — in a social space. Freedom, so conceived, will no longer be a pure notion. It will be intermixed with various other elements including the so-called mutually conflicting elements of freedom, such as, freedom and determinism. As a result, freedom will not have a determinate meaning. It will be ambiguous in terms of its meaning and significance. In view of this, it is all the more essential to find out the nature of freedom in constructive terms. In our assessment, authenticity is the core of freedom. It defines the nature of freedom. If freedom is

---

16. C. Smith, "The Notion of Object in the Phenomenology of Merleau-Ponty", *Philosophy*, Vol. 3-4, 1964, p. 111.

understood as authenticity then much of ambiguity around freedom can be removed. But one must be clear here that authenticity should not be understood in absolute terms. Authenticity is thus not the total negation of inauthenticity. It is due to the complexity of human existence that one finds the coexistence of conflicting things together. In our earlier discussion on freedom we have seen how freedom and mechanical part of human behaviour (i.e., sedimentation of automatic skills and habits) both exist together. In fact, the latter provides the background to more conscious and innovative thought and action. Hence, there is no pure freedom. In a similar way there is no pure authenticity. Authenticity is a matter of degree that can be achieved on the ground of inauthenticity.

Coming to the notion of authenticity the best way to understand it will be to see it in the light of the difference between true and false feeling. True and false feeling may be seen as authentic and inauthentic feeling. In the phenomenological-existentialist tradition this aspect of human existence has been discussed at a great length. In my presentation, I shall follow the similar line of thinking especially that of Merleau-Ponty and Sartre. Merleau-Ponty[17] thus explains the difference between authentic and inauthentic feeling by citing the example of true and false love. False love is not unreal; but it is not concerned with the wholeness of being. It is thus concerned only with a part — the part lying at the level of the periphery of my existence. As a result, the large part of my being is untouched by the superficial emotion of love. In false love I do not love the person as what he is or she is. I see the person in my own light — in the light of my own consideration and feeling. In false love, thus, I project my own feeling on the person whom I love. But such a love cannot last long because there is nothing intrinsic in it. It will disappear as soon as I change — as soon as my feeling will be changed. It is a situation where loving a person means loving some qualities

17. M. Merleau-Ponty, *The Primacy of Perception and other Essays*, pp. 377-83.

of the person (e.g., the eyes of a woman). Whereas, in true love, as Sartre observes, my emotion discloses the object of my love to me. I will love a person because he/she is lovable.

Inauthentic love or for that matter inauthentic emotions are superficial. They do not touch the centre of our being. They are more with the periphery of our existence in the same way habits, conventions and mechanical behaviour are. In inauthentic emotions I do not see myself — my own being. This creates fragmentation within me.

I have said that inauthenticity is not unreal nor is it a total negation of authenticity. In existential term, they are not polar opposites. The conflict between the two may be understood as one (authenticity) being threatened by the other (inauthenticity).

Authenticity is a kind of self-revelation. In self-revelation we come know about ourselves — what we are and what we are doing. But self-revelation is possible only when we have self-knowledge. Self-knowledge is the basis of self-revelation. Unless, I am aware of my true feelings I cannot act authentically. But this is where the problem lies since we cannot have a clear knowledge about ourselves. Merleau-Ponty[18] points out that we know ourselves in an ambiguous way. This happens due to various reasons. First, to have self-knowledge means to be conscious of myself — to be conscious of my emotions and feelings. For to achieve this must be absolutely transparent which is not possible due to the peculiar nature of consciousness. It is due to its transcendent nature consciousness loses itself in things of the world. But consciousness can know itself only be withdrawing from the world. Consciousness cannot do both at the same time. As a result, it can be vaguely aware of itself while getting involved with this world. Second, self-knowledge, to a great extent, is achieved through indirect way. I came to know myself through other people. They have their own understanding and assessment about myself. They show me — what I am. Third,

18. *The Primacy of Perception and other Essays*, p. 296.

there are occasions where I know myself after the event is over. This shows while I am living through an event I cannot have clear knowledge of myself. Finally, language can be misleading in achieving self-knowledge. It is through language I come to know and identify my feeling. But language can also hide my own feelings from myself. Words and phrases may be inadequate to express my feelings properly. As Merleau-Ponty observes, I may have certain feeling inside but there is no expression to name it. As a result, I lack proper knowledge of it.

As we can see there cannot be any complete self-revelation. Self-revelation which is based on self-knowledge is itself not complete since thus degrees of self-revelation depending on the nature of knowledge attained by the agent. In view of this, the relationship between authenticity and inauthenticity may be said to be a matter of different degrees of self-revelation achieved by a person.

If authenticity is self-revelation inauthenticity must be self-deception. Self-deception comes when I do not reveal myself through my action. What is revealed may be superficial feeling hiding the true nature of feeling. For example, in view of my friend's death I may not be feeling sad, but I superficially express my sadness. This is an inauthentic behaviour and I am doing it due to the pressure of my community outside. The same is with false love. I love a woman not because she is lovable but I love her because I want her property. All these actions suggest that they do not come spontaneously from the agent. They do not touch the entire being of the person. They only affect the periphery of his being. The extreme case of self-deception is one where a person is aware of this contradiction between the two feelings but refuses to recognise this knowledge and, in turn, adopts a forced attitude thus showing his sadness to others. It is, indeed, an ambivalent situation involving the two states of my existence. At one level, authenticity is recognised and at another level it is denied. A typical example of it is Sartre's example of a woman in bad faith. On the one hand, the woman wants to be treated by her companion as a free person and not as a sexual object. But, on the other hand, since she could reconcile these two attitudes she allows herself to be treated as a sexual object[19]. She forced herself to adopt this attitude and managed to forget the other. Finally, there is a clarification. It is true that inauthenticity and self-deception are closely related but the former has a wider meaning than the latter. An action may be inauthentic though there may not be any self-deception. It is inauthentic from the point of view higher values. The woman in Sartre's example may resolve the conflict and may decide to be treated as a sexual object. Thus, there will be no self-deception. But this action will be still inauthentic because by allowing her to be treated in this manner she prevents herself to grow as a free independent subject. From the point of view of higher values this action is inauthentic. It is only through a committed action that one can be authentic.

We have come to the end of our mapping of the domain constituted by freedom. The concept of freedom has been unduly influenced by the doctrine of fact/value dichotomy. As a result, the existential nature of freedom is overlooked. Freedom is not conceived in situational terms. The main spirit behind our mapping of freedom is to restore the existential nature of freedom with the help of a supporting methodology involving fact/value holism. In constructive term, the ethics of human freedom consists in authenticity. It lies in my authentic behaviour where I can be said to be true to myself.

---

19. J.P. Sartre, *Being and Nothingness*, Methuen, London, 1969, pp. 55-6.

4

Moral Personhood

S.K. Mohanty

THE expression 'moral personhood' has been used to express several different ideas. It has been used to signify the class of individuals who can be treated as the proper objects of moral concern and sympathy. The expression has also been used to delineate a class of individuals who ought to be accorded dignity and autonomy. There is a further use of the expression that conveys the idea that persons are agents who are morally accountable. I shall try to argue that these notions of moral personhood are distinct ideas. One can be a person in the first or second sense without being a person in the third sense. In other words, someone can be an object of moral concern without being a responsible moral agent. B.H. Boruah and R.C. Pradhan, in their contributions to this volume, have elaborated the concept of a person that signifies rational moral agency. The two other senses of moral personhood are also significant from the moral point of view. These different senses should be kept separate, because there is always the danger of treating different concepts as a single concept when the same expression is employed to express different concepts. There is also the danger of drawing unwarranted conclusions by using the expression in one sense in one premise and in another sense in the other premise. I wish to analyse and bring to focus some of the issues related to the notions of personhood from the standpoint of moral concern.

Some philosophers believe that only moral agents are the

proper objects of moral concern. In support of this it can be maintained that 'duty' and 'right' being relative and complementary terms, only responsible moral agents can claim to be holders of moral rights. However, 'duty implies rights is' true in the sense that if someone has a right then some others have a corresponding duty. This claim is different from the assertion that if an individual has a right, then that person must have duties as well. One can be an object of moral concern without being a moral subject. This claim may be questioned on the ground that rights and duties being reciprocal, if a creature lacks duties and obligations, it cannot also have rights. According to the contract tradition reciprocity is the basis of morality. It has been argued that morality has its origin in the contract between people for their mutual benefit. I should not harm others because they in turn can appreciate my restraint and reciprocate appropriately. Only creatures that can recompense can have moral claims on me. There are, however, serious objections to this theory[1]. If our moral concern to others is based on the sense of reciprocity people possess, then our moral concern will vary in proportion to the degree of sensibility these people have. Further, among human beings there are infants, small children, the mentally retarded who may not possess any sense of justice, reciprocity or give-and-take. A contract theory will exclude such beings from the scope of moral concern and sympathy. The theory will also exclude the future generation, as they do not exist now to enter into even tacit agreement. There are also adult human beings lacking a sense of reciprocity and they will also have to be excluded from the scope of our moral concerns. The theory will seriously restrict the scope of moral concern and reduce morality to a sort of club membership. Thus we shall have to give up the theory that only persons who are morally responsible are proper objects of moral concern.

Consider the idea of a person as a proper object of moral

1. P. Singer, *Practical Ethics*, 2nd edn., (Cambridge University Press, 1993) p. 18 ff.

concern and sympathy. The concept of a person is often elucidated by contrasting it with the idea of property. To view someone as a person is not to regard that individual as a property, object or possession. A property is a possession that has utility value for those who need it. Things like cars and houses are possessions. These can be valuable for some. These have instrumental value. Persons too may have instrumental value, but our attitude towards persons is not exhausted by whatever utility value they have. Our moral attitude to persons contains a sense of duty to treat such beings as ends and not merely as means. It reflects the recognition that persons are beings who have moral rights.

Why should one recognise that persons have moral worth? The suggestion that personhood is the basis of moral status is not very illuminating because the supposed explanation will be circular. We first say that human beings have moral rights because they are persons. To the question, what it is to be a person, if the answer is that to be a person is, among other things, to have inherent worth, then the answer will be circular. The concept of person is normative, but one can always ask for the ground or justification for assigning the normative status to persons.

One who subscribes to a theory of objective values might argue that persons have objective value. In this view the moral concern for the well-being of the individuals can be grounded in their inherent objective worth. This theory, however, suffers from serious limitations. It is a form of moral realism. Like any other metaphysical theory, this suffers from its inherent weakness that if one refuses to subscribe to this metaphysical theory, we have no means for settling the dispute. Another alternative could be a form of value naturalism, but this would again involve the naturalistic fallacy of reducing values to natural properties. In the face of these difficulties in theories advocating objectivity of value, it has been the practice among philosophers to embrace some form of value relativism or subjectivity of values. Value subjectivism, however, is not a very comfortable position as it flies in the face of common sense view of morality.

The concept of value has two dimensions and correspondingly it can be construed in two ways. Value can mean 'values people hold' or it can mean 'the value something has'. In the former sense, value is an activity and it is the activity of a rational mind that makes value judgements. In this sense values are subjective, being dependent on value-projecting beings. In the latter sense, value has reference to the things that have value. Values, however, cannot be objective in the same sense in which facts are objective. Values are not facts. A statement of fact is an assertion, whereas a value judgement is an activity. None the less, values have reference to something beyond the valuing subject. Even though values are not facts, values must be 'informed' by the facts about the object valued. We in fact figure out moral prescriptions from descriptive facts. We do not make things valuable by valuing them as we do not make statements true by believing them[2]. Values point to something beyond the valuing mind. The content of a value judgement has reference to the features of the thing that is valued. Values cannot be subjective in the sense in which an individual's beliefs in the existence of ghosts, witches or unicorns are subjective. Such beliefs are purely subjective in so far as ghosts, witches and unicorns have no existence. Thus, value is a function which involves both a subject that values and the object that is valued. 'Value' in this respect resembles 'meaning'. Nigel remarks that the meaning of an utterance depends in part on what happens in the mind of the person who utters it, and more importantly it also depends on what goes on in other people's mind and what goes on between people. Nigel remarks that the meaningfulness of language is also a social and not a purely internal, mental matter[3]. Similar

2. R.M. Hare, "Moral Reasoning about the Environment" in Almond, B and Hill, D (eds.), *Applied Philosophy*: *morals and metaphysics in contemporary debate* (London, Routledge, 1991), p. 12.

3. J.T. Nigel, "Zombi Killer" in R.H. Steward, *et al* (eds.), *Toward a Science of Consciousness II*: *The Second Tucson Discussions and Debates* (Cambridge, MA, the M.I.T. Press, 1998).

remarks can also be made with regard to value. An acceptable theory of value must maintain equal distance from both subjectivism and objectivism in the traditional sense of these terms.

As I pointed out earlier, the expression 'moral personhood' has been used to signify the status of beings that are proper objects of moral concern. There are two basic issues with regard to our moral concern. These are issues concerning the ground and scope of moral concern. The starting point of ethical concern adopted by an individual is bound to be that individual's own interests and desires. But in moral judgement one goes beyond the personal point of view. As I value my own interests, others who are like me in relevant respects must also be valuing their interests. Sentient beings have interest in the relief from pain, interest in the satisfaction of desires and needs. They feel happy when their desires are fulfilled and unhappy when desires are thwarted. As ethics takes a universal point of view, one ought to acknowledge that an interest is an interest irrespective of whose interest it is. If pain is undesirable, it must be undesirable for everyone who has interest in relief from it. It is interesting to note that both Kantian and utilitarian theories agree on the importance of the role of universalisability in ethics. Moral philosophers apply the Golden Rule, in some form or other, to determine the scope of our moral concern. If my welfare matters, so does the welfare of any conscious being.

Only sentient beings can have interest in any morally significant sense, because the capacity for suffering and enjoying is a prerequisite for having interest. Sentient beings have sense experience, feel pleasure and pain, enjoy and suffer. These beings are active agents in so far as they acquire information about the environment and exert influence on the environment on the basis of the information acquired. They too have the 'will-to-live'. They are subjects of experience and have phenomenal consciousness. There is 'something it is like' to be in a particular phenomenal state. A phenomenal mental state has a distinctive subjective character. Apart from human beings, higher animals have desires, beliefs, expectations and feelings like love and affection. If we treat human beings as moral subjects, then logical consistency demands that we treat non-human animals from the moral point of view. This requires that moral concern will have to be understood in a broad sense so as to include within its scope all human beings and non-human animals who possess the capacity to feel pain and pleasure irrespective of their level of intelligence, reasoning capacity, ability to reciprocate and the like. From the point of view of moral concern what matters is the fact that conscious beings have interest. As universality of concern is built into the very fabric of our ethical consideration, we cannot ignore any being that satisfies the minimal conditions of being a moral subject or person. Moral concern for sentient animals becomes more persuasive when we reflect on the following hypothetical situation. Imagine that some aliens, who are far superior to us in intelligence, invade the earth. How would we like them to treat us? If we would like them to treat us fairly, we should also treat the non-human animals with appropriate moral concern. One can also imagine oneself in the place of a sentient being who is morally abused and ask how one would like to be treated by others.

The nature of moral concern appropriate to sentient beings can be compared with parental love. Both involve a personal stance, an attitude of concern and care. This personal stance is different from the personal stance appropriate to persons as moral agents who are morally accountable. As parental love is not proportionate to the child's talent or any other useful trait, moral concern is not proportional to the individual's personal traits. As the disadvantaged child deserves greater parental care, the disadvantaged members of the moral community can merit greater moral concern. Therefore, a greater concern for the disadvantaged does not go against the principle of equal consideration of interest. However, moral concern, unlike parental love, is grounded in reason, which gives it its universal and normative status. Reason commands that like cases are treated alike. This demand is a demand of rational consistency.

The nature of our moral concern, however, will largely depend upon our idea of personhood and what we value in persons. An individual values her happiness or well-being. In the case of human beings this happiness cannot be identified with seeking pleasure and avoiding pain. Satisfaction of basic biological needs is no doubt a part of what we value in our life and it is a prerequisite for having higher interests. Human beings have qualitatively higher interests. Mill has rightly held that it is better to be a man dissatisfied than a pig satisfied. What it really means is that the conception of human satisfaction is not the same as satisfaction an animal seeks. Human welfare involves more than having pleasure and avoiding pain. Human beings have the capacity to judge and value. Mill says,

> Of two pleasures, if there be one to which all or almost all who have experience of both give a decided preference, irrespective of any feeling of moral obligation to prefer it, that is the more desirable pleasure. If one of the two is, by those who are competently acquainted with both, placed so far above the other that they prefer it, even though knowing it to be attended with a greater amount of discontent, and would not resign it for any quantity of the other pleasure which their nature is capable of, we are justified in ascribing to the preferred enjoyment a superiority in quality so far outweighing quantity as to render it, in comparison, of small account.
>
> – *Utilitarianism* ch. 2, para 5

Human beings prefer qualitatively higher pleasures even at the cost of discontent or suffering. Judging pleasure as lower and higher involves value judgements and the application of higher faculty of reason. Mill's preference for utilitarianism very well explains the moral value of rational preference. We would not get a correct account of human welfare if we strip away rational preferences or what rationally matters to the individual. As freedom is a precondition for the exercise of rational preference, human dignity and freedom has to be acknowledged as having moral worth. If human beings differ from non-human animals in pursuing a dignified life, our moral concern for human beings cannot be the same for both human and non-human animals. In addition to physical well-being, the basic human interests can be grouped under broad categories like freedom for self-expression, companionship and knowledge. Human beings are thus morally entitled to make life-plans of their own, to fix their own goals and decide on the means to achieve these goals. The Universal Declaration of Human Rights by the United Nations sets out in great detail what these rights are. The important point to note here is that these rights are not based on actual possession of distinct human qualities and traits in any significant proportion. The fact is that human beings differ in a variety of ways. For instance, some are great planners, but some are driven by circumstances, by short-term goals. People have gradable traits like talent, skill, character, personality, etc. None of these traits, either separately or collectively, can serve as the basis of moral concern. The basis has to be the common interest, the common humanity which human beings share with each other. Persons are self-conscious beings who are aware of their existence over time. As ethics takes a universal point of view, our moral concern will include not only rational moral agents who are persons in a stronger sense of the term, but also individuals who have the relevant potentiality to develop. Consider the case of a human child who has not developed into a responsible moral agent. Edgar Page, in a different context, draws attention to a large difference in attitude to gametes and embryos, on the one hand, and to children, on the other[4]. The manner in which sperms, gametes or embryos can be donated or transferred, children cannot be so transferred. At the background of this distinction in attitude we can discern a contrast between objects, on the one hand and human persons, on the other. Persons, unlike commodities, have intrinsic moral worth. The morally appropriate concern in the context of human beings involves the recognition of the dignity of the person and respect for autonomy. A person is a rational self-conscious agent. It is desirable that such a person directs his own life. However, when a human individual lacks the ability and potentiality to develop uniquely human qualities she would not be excluded from the scope of moral concern. She will still

---

4. "Donation, Surrogacy and Adoption" in Almond and Hill (eds.) *ibid.*, p. 278.

have interest in the relief from pain and interest in her well-being. This shows that the two concepts 'person' and 'human being' are not synonymous. We must admit of the possibility that there can be non-human persons as well as human beings that are not persons. But at the same time it has to be acknowledged that any exclusion of a member of the species *homo sapiens* from the status of persons will have to be minimal for the purpose of assigning moral worth.

As a human being I value or prefer certain things in my life. In fact, a rational self-conscious being will prefer to live a life of dignity and respect. So we should value these qualities in all creatures that are similar to us in having the capacity for pursuing these interests. Our moral concern for human beings can be grounded on the universal maxim that equals be treated equally. The starting point in ethical reasoning is the individual who values her own interests. Reason requires that we treat like cases alike. If my interest has value, persons who are similar to me in having interests must also have similar worth. An interest is an interest irrespective of whose interest it is. Thus reason enables the moral agent to transcend the self-interest and adopt the universal concern. Reason also enables us in recognising the social nature of human interest.

I have attempted to provide an outline of the two different senses of moral personhood based on the two kinds of moral concern. These notions of personhood are different from the idea of personhood as a moral agent. The idea of a moral patient does not entail the idea of moral agent. The first type of moral concern encompasses all subjects of experience who have the capacity of feeling pain and pleasure. This is the community of sentient beings, which includes human beings as well. All sentient beings have interest in their well-being and feel frustrated when their interests are thwarted. Since pain is undesirable irrespective of whose pain it is, this interest is the same in all the sentient beings. In so far as sentient beings are self-valuers who value their own interests, they can be said to have inherent value. Since sentient beings are subjects of experience, self-valuers and can have reasons for actions in the form of desires and beliefs, these beings constitute a moral community and members of this community as holders of moral rights can be said to possess moral personhood. There is a stronger notion of moral personhood that applies to human persons. Human beings not only value their interests they also have value preferences. In addition to interests in their welfare human beings have the capacity to formulate and follow norms. Dignity and autonomy of the human individual are preconditions for the manifestation of human worth. The same universalisability maxim that enables a moral agent to recognise the equal worth of interests of sentient subjects also convinces her to recognise the equal worth of the dignity and freedom of all rational beings. The recognition of fundamental human rights as well as animal rights involves recognition of moral worth of beings.

Moral valuation is the activity of rational agents. So it is distinctly a human activity. Non-human animals value their own interests and human beings too value their interests, which are qualitatively different from interests of animals. Human beings as moral agents have the capacity for self-transcendence and the ability to recognise value in others. Their reflective self-transcendence is a product of reason. Reason gives the human beings the status of moral agent. It is only humans who recognise the trans-subjective values. The realisation that other beings value themselves as one values oneself and that it is the same value that is valued by different creatures lead to the recognition of intrinsic value. The notion of moral agency thus involves a stronger criterion of personhood.

Rationality, consciousness, self-consciousness, intelligence, a sense of the past and the future, the capacity to relate to other, concern for others are some of the features which persons have. All these features are gradable and actual persons possess these features in different proportions. Further, personhood is a cluster concept. Wittgenstein's notion of family resemblance comes handy in understanding the nature of personhood. Presence of some of these features entitles a being the status of a person, but absence of any of these does not disqualify an individual from that status. Further, for the purpose ascribing either animal rights or even human rights we need to relax the criterion of personhood substantially. To attribute moral concern to sentient beings, all we need is the fact that sentient beings are subjects of phenomenal experience. For ascribing human rights we need a stronger criterion that recognises the ability of humans to pursue qualitatively higher value, the ability for value choice. In such cases the requirement that the beings have phenomenal consciousness can be relaxed. Even if a human child is born with the disorder such that she cannot feel pain but has other person-making properties we cannot withdraw her from the status of a person. There is an interesting episode of Star Trek: The Next Generation ("The Measure of Man"). In the Star Ship Enterprise the scientist who created an android (Commander Data) wants to dismantle Data. But Commander Data claims that he is a person. Data has intelligence and self-awareness, Data also values things and has preferences. Data too has representational states corresponding to our desires and beliefs. But Data lacks inner experience, phenomenal consciousness. There is nothing that it is like to be that machine. Data, however, can have higher-order thoughts to monitor the lower level representational states. After the hearing the court gives the ruling that Commander Data is a person and has the freedom to choose. In the above cases, the case of a human child who is partially blind and the case of Data who is completely blind in respect of phenomenal consciousness, we feel constrained to assign them the status of a person, although in different senses of the term.

When we view persons as moral agents the conditions for the application of the concept of person have to be stricter. In order to be a moral agent it is not sufficient that the person has the potentiality for rational choice or the ability to entertain second order desires. A person in order to be a moral agent must actually possess these features in substantial measure, so that notions of accountability and responsibility can meaningfully be applied to them.

The Contributors

Dr. Bijoy H. Boruah is Professor of Philosophy in the Department of Humanities and Social Sciences of the I.I.T., Kanpur. Professor Boruah specialises in Philosophy of Mind, Moral Philosophy and Philosophical Aesthetics.

Dr. Ramesh Chandra Pradhan is Professor of Philosophy at the Central University of Hyderabad. He is specialist in the Philosophy of Wittgenstein, Philosophy of Language and Moral Philosophy.

Dr. Amitabha Das Gupta is Professor of Philosophy at the Central University of Hyderabad. His areas of specialisation include Philosophy of Language, Philosophy of Science and Moral Philosophy.

Dr. Saroj Kumar Mohanty, the editor of this volume, is Reader in Philosophy at Utkal University. His main areas of specialisation are Philosophy of Mind, Philosophy of Values and Practical Ethics.